Raising a Reader

ALSO BY JENNIE NASH

Altared States

The Victoria's Secret Catalog Never Stops Coming

Jennie Nash

St. Martin's Press ≋ New York

Raising

a Reader

A Mother's Tale of
Desperation and Delight

www.stmartins.com

Library of Congress Cataloging-in-Publication Data

Nash, Jennie.
  Raising a reader : a mother's tale of desperation and delight / Jennie Nash.—1st ed.
    p. cm.
  ISBN 0-312-31534-1
  1. Children—Books and reading. 2. Reading—Parent participation. I. Title.

Z1037.A1N157 2003
028.5'5—dc21

                                                         2003041397

First Edition: August 2003

10   9   8   7   6   5   4   3   2   1

For my mom and my dad

Contents

The mother's heart is the child's schoolroom.

—HENRY WARD BEECHER

Raising a Reader

Introduction

Learning to read has become big business in our get-to-the-finish-line-first culture. There are electronic games to teach reading, after-school programs to improve reading, special books to encourage reading, and tests to measure whether or not children are reading at the appropriate time in the appropriate manner.

From a certain perspective, this is good news. Reading is, after all, one of life's most useful skills. It's what we all need to be able to fill out an employment application, understand a menu, follow a road sign, and decide what the headlines of the newspaper mean. It's how we learn about the progress of a disease, the politics of war, and how to make pastry dough; and there is no doubt that it should be at the top of the list of education's objectives. Reading is also, of course, one of the most exciting, entertaining, enriching, enjoyable things you can do on a Wednesday evening, a summer vacation, or an airplane flight to Chicago. You can find companionship in books, counsel, solace, and delight. You can spend hours alone in a room listening to the quiet music of the written word, transported completely to another time and place.

But reading suffers when we turn it into a high-anxiety, competitive activity. The process suffers, our kids suffer, and we suffer along with them. I know this, not because I have any expertise in teaching reading beyond my own experience as a parent, but because during the years in which my two children learned how to read, there were many times when my desire for them to succeed strayed into desperation, my hope morphed into obsession, and instead of helping pass on my passion, my resolve got in the way. The magic moments—the ones in which my own love of reading was naturally passed on—came in their own sweet time, through the blessing of being together in the presence of good books and by the grace needed to see each of my children as individuals separate from me.

Like so many of the things we do as parents, raising readers happens in bursts of delight and desperation, in the push and pull of digging in and letting go, day in and day out, both because of and in spite of our efforts. What I've set about doing in this book is to examine all the elements—positive, negative, planned, and accidental—that went into building the literary life of the two little people I know best. My hope is to share how it works and to show why it's worth it.

1

Passion

If I had to choose the one thing I wish for my children above all others, I'd have to say that I wish they will find and pursue a passion, something they love so much they can build a life on it. I've been blessed in my career as a writer, and I can't imagine giving over my days to work that feels like drudgery or duty or worse. I believe my job as a parent is to expose my kids to the things that they might fall in love with: here's what dancing looks like, this is what throwing clay feels like, this is what doctors do. My kids' job is to take it all in and listen to what speaks to their hearts.

It's easy to recognize when someone feels passionate about something, whether you're talking to someone, reading a description of what they love, or watching them work or perform, because it's such an attractive characteristic. It's the reason we cheer when the heartfelt performer wins the Olympic Gold Medal over the steely technician. It's the reason we can't look away when a little kid stands on a stage and belts out the "National Anthem" for all he's worth. But you don't have to be famous or in the spotlight for passion to shine through.

My mom, for example, loves music, and you can hear her passion every time she talks about it even if you have no clue what music or musicians she's referring to. She recently wrote me an e-mail about a performance of the Los Angeles Philharmonic:

> Esa-Pekka Salonen brought his band to Santa Barbara tonight and played one of the most memorable concerts in my hearing. The thing was Mahler's Symphony #1. We've all heard it, or pieces of it, 4,500 times. But never like this. What a *thrilling* concert!!! I was in tears at the end because of the brilliance, the discipline to make it pretty perfect for a live performance. E-P is a study: I sit in the last row (on purpose) with binoculars. Every muscle in his body moves with each demand: I'm certain his toes do as well.

My mom's excitement is infectious. I want to hear Esa-Pekka Salonen conduct the Los Angeles Philharmonic, even though I'm not a big fan of that kind of music. And I want to grab the phone to call my mom and tell her that she made me smile.

Once when I was reading a book of essays by adventurous men, I came across an entry by a pilot named Bruce Rodger. I don't have any particular feeling for flying, and I had no idea who Bruce Rodger was, but I instantly knew exactly what he meant, and I instantly decided I liked him. He wrote:

My thought processes, my brain, my hands, my vision, my hearing—when I was in the air, they all connected and I had this feeling of oneness with the plane. I have it every time I'm in the cockpit. God gave me a gift to pilot airplanes. I was born to fly.

What were my kids born to do? That is the question I hope to help them answer. And because reading is the thing I love most, it's only natural for me to hope it will become something they love, too.

All parents want their children to share what they love. You can feel their heightened sense of hope in the stands at Little League games and on the folding seats of piano recitals. You can see it backstage before the performance of *The Nutcracker* each year at Christmas. That hope is the driving force behind family businesses of every shape and size—the notion that the child will grow up to love the very same thing that the parent has loved. It's exciting enough to think about sharing what you love best in the world with the people you love best in the world, but to imagine that that they, too, will grow up to adopt it as their passion is to dream of magic.

Although I always liked to read, I didn't realize how much I loved it until after my graduation from college—after I'd earned a degree in English by reading and interpreting thousands of pages of mostly American literature and taken a job as an editorial assistant at Ballantine Books in New York City. Even though I was engaged in the business of words and writing, I found that I missed being a reader of the right book at the right time. There's such a big difference between reading a book because you have to in order to write a term paper or an editorial report and reading a book because you stumbled across it, selected it, and found that it grabbed you by the shoulders and wouldn't let you go.

Edward Abbey's *Desert Solitaire* grabbed me because it was the first argument I ever read that seemed like it could move mountains and because I glimpsed in it some of the fire that fueled my dad, the environmentalist, and his never-ending need to escape to wild country. Zora Neale Hurson's *Their Eyes Were Watching God* entranced me before I got married because the love between Hurston's characters in that story—though as different in circumstance as you could possibly get from my own—described the overpowering way I felt about my husband-to-be. *Bird by Bird* by Anne Lamott inspires me on a regular basis because it makes me laugh and it makes me want to write. The short stories of Andre Dubus and Alice Munro comfort me whenever I read them because they make me feel that redemption is at hand for all our human failings.

Writer-director Nora Ephron describes the experience of the reader as a kind of bliss, and I think she gets it just right:

I've just surfaced from spending several days in a state of rapture. I was reading a book. I loved this book. I loved every second of it. I was transported into its world. I was reminded of all sorts of things in my own life. I was in anguish over the fate of its characters. I felt alive and engaged and positively brilliant, bursting with ideas, brimming with memories of other books I've loved. . . . I'm truly beside myself with joy.

My children, Carlyn and Emily, who are now ten and seven, have shared many book-filled moments with me that have that sense of magic about them. My favorite times are when we read together after dinner, when the duties of the day are gone. I don't read to the kids so much anymore, but side by side *with* them—me reading my book, they reading theirs. We often read this way in my big bed, under the heavy weight of blankets. I might be reading a biography of Rachel Carson, one of my daughters might be reading *The Fairy Rebel*. Her toes curl up against mine for warmth, and the only sound is the turning of pages and the occasional question—"What does 'chaos' mean?" "How do you say 'intricate'?" We are together in our shared enjoyment of words, but immersed in separate worlds. We are exactly what I hoped we would be: a family of readers.

HOW TO GET CAUGHT READING

Learn-to-read experts are always talking about how you should make sure your kids catch you reading so that they see that it's an activity you enjoy and value. Since the majority of my reading happens when I am in bed and my kids are asleep, I always wondered how to pull this off. I came up with two simple solutions: One is to spend some time reading with my kids, as I described above, at their bedtime. I leave the dinner dishes in the sink, I don't return phone calls, and I pick up a book instead. I just move my reading time forward. In other words, if I'm reading a story to the kids, I finish that, then pick up my own book and read silently for a few minutes as they read silently to themselves.

The other solution is to urge your kids to bring a book with them when they come into your bedroom on weekend mornings. Snuggle them next to you and read a few pages of your own book while they page through theirs. It's a sweet ritual that packs a big message. On days when the kids are home sick, you can take this idea and make a whole morning of it: Bring in some tea or ginger ale and a huge stack of books. Read them a few books, then suggest they look at one while you read a few pages of your book.

2

Obsession

Passion can be so close to obsession that it's easy to step over the line. There's a man at my gym who is waiting for his son to become a professional tennis player. I see them—a boy of about ten and his solemn dad—hauling baskets of balls and bags of rackets to the tennis courts at all times of day and night, in all kinds of weather. When they get out onto the court, the boy stands on the baseline and the dad stands on the other side of the net and throws him tennis balls and marching orders. The boy is very good. He's won some big tournaments. He has a top ranking. He probably enjoys his time on the court and his time with his dad, and he may even nurture a vision of himself as a champion. But it's clear from the boy's grim determination that the dad believes the whole universe depends on his son's success in this sport.

I know there are many parents who are naturally more patient and open minded about their desires for their children—my husband among them. Rob loved being a swimmer. He said he always felt free and clearheaded in the water, and he savors the feeling to this day. Does he want our children to become competitive swimmers? It would delight him no end. But he did not throw them into the water to teach them how to swim when they were three. He has not dragged them to swim meets or forced them to watch Olympic trials on late-night cable TV. If our children found peace and happiness in another sport—or in playing the violin or building cabinets—Rob would be as pleased.

Although I can see the wisdom in Rob's reasonable stance, I also recognize in myself the less-forgiving impulse of the tennis-playing dad. I have demonstrated it more times than I'd like to admit. Reading is a particularly slippery passion to want to pass along because it's a skill that most parents would agree their children *have* to master, to one degree or another. It's part of the basic kid curriculum; so if you're pushing reading, you're not being a pushy parent, you're just doing your job. The problem with pushing so hard, however, is that I never stopped to consider that if left alone with a normal amount of support and encouragement my children might have ended up in exactly the same place, readingwise, as they did under the white-hot heat of my passion. I never stopped and wondered whether you can, or should even try, to make someone *love* to do anything. I just plowed ahead, putting a love of books so high on the list of what mattered most that I sometimes put it above the kids themselves.

My worst offense occurred when Carlyn, my oldest daughter, was still years away from the age of reading. She was two, so she was frequently angry at me for some seemingly small infraction, such as suggesting the wrong color socks to wear or suggesting she even wear socks in the first place. On this particular occasion she was angry about a book. She wanted to keep looking at the book instead of putting on her socks, so instead of simply throwing a fit, which was her usual routine, she looked at me and ripped one of the pages in half

I yelped. The little book she had so callously torn was older than I was. Several generations of readers in my family had preserved it all these years, and it was in my hands, on my watch, that this horrible thing had happened. My child had defaced a family heirloom out of spite! Out of vengeance!

"We do not tear books!" I cried, as if she had yanked the cat's tail or taken a bite out of a playmate. I stormed out to the garage and hauled in two large cardboard boxes. While Carlyn continued sitting on the floor, stunned into submission, I loaded in all the books from the shelves in her bedroom. I piled in *Where's Spot?* and *Paddington Takes a Bath, Hop on Pop,* and *Richard Scarry's Best Balloon Ride Ever.* In went *Winnie the Pooh* and all the little white Beatrix Potter books about chipmunks and rabbits and hedgehogs.

When the boxes were full, I sat on the floor and took Carlyn in my lap. I knew that what I was about to do would hurt her, and despite my fury, I wanted to soften the blow. "I'm taking these books away for three days," I explained, "because if you can't take care of your books, you can't have them to look at."

Carlyn began to cry, although it wasn't clear whether she was crying over the books or crying over her mother, who had clearly snapped in some profound and fearful way.

There wasn't enough room in the boxes to hold all the books on the little wooden bookshelf, but it seemed important to take away every book, so I went back out to the garage and got down the red-and-white Coleman Cooler we use for camping trips. In went Shel Silverstein's book of poems and *Big Black Bear*. In went *Cinderella* and *Wombat Stew*. Within minutes, I had the boxes and the cooler filled and locked behind the closet door in my office at the end of the hall.

Carlyn wailed as I worked, and she wailed as I took out the Scotch tape and repaired the damaged page as best as I could, matching up the ragged edges of the tear. When I was done, I went back to Carlyn's room and gently suggested that we put on her socks so we could get out of the house and go to the park.

The book Carlyn tore was *Chicken Soup with Rice*. It was a miniature version, just two by three inches. It was bound in red fabric, with gold letters spelling out the title. It was one in a set of three books. Inside each of them was one short, perfect little story by Maurice Sendak—*Chicken Soup with Rice, One Was Johnny,* and *Alligators All Around*. I have no idea how I came to be the owner of these little red books. I can't remember being presented with them, or asking for them, or discovering them among the boxes of old pictures and decks of cards that came out of Grandma Nash's house when she died during my senior year in college. I simply owned the little red books that I knew had been hers, and I loved them.

My dad could recite *Chicken Soup with Rice* verse for verse— along with "The Cremation of Sam McGee" and "The Midnight

Ride of Paul Revere." It's easy to understand how he could have memorized the story because after only a few readings, Carlyn and I could recite verses, as well:

In January
it's so nice
while slipping
on the sliding ice
to sip hot chicken soup
with rice.
Sipping once
sipping twice
sipping chicken soup
with rice.

It's almost impossible not to get those rhythms stuck in your head, and Sendak clearly banks on this. We've probably said his lines from *Where the Wild Things Are* a million times—"I'll eat you up, I love you so / And Max said no." Once an author's language becomes part of your own, you're hooked for life.

The boxes of banned books stayed in my office closet for the three days I'd prescribed. At bedtime every night, Carlyn would ask if we could read a book; and when I reminded her that the books were gone, she would wail as if the hurt were brand new. I missed the stories as much as she did. I missed the ritual of a book at the end of the day, the calm of sitting down, the chance to sink into those familiar rhythms. It was almost as if I didn't know what to do with my child if I couldn't read to her. We tried to sing or to talk instead, but it wasn't the same.

When the books finally came out on the morning of the third day, we celebrated. We examined each book as we took it out of the box, naming characters and reciting favorite lines. We smiled and we laughed. When all the books were back on the shelf, I brought back *Chicken Soup with Rice,* and showed Carlyn where I had taped the page back together.

"See? It's OK," I said, "It's all better. But let's not ever hurt a book like that again," I said.

"I won't, Mama," she promised, and nodded, and took the little red book and put it on her shelf next to the other two books in the set.

I've since learned that the three little red books were part of a set called the *Nutshell Library,* which originally included four books. The last book—the one missing from our set—was a book called *Pierre: A Cautionary Tale in Five Chapters and a Prologue.* I was thrilled that someone—not ME!—had lost the fourth book and the slipcase the set had come in. This made it easier to forgive Carlyn for tearing the book and to forgive myself for flying into such a rage.

Kids are human. We expect them to make mistakes—to tear the pages of cherished books, shove mashed potatoes into the CD player, and snip off their ponytails with the long-handled orange scissors. But parents are human as well, and if we care a great deal about something—anything—we're bound not to behave as well as we'd like. I never hauled the books away again, but I did other things just as rash. Fortunately for me and for my kids, my mistakes existed within a larger spirit of abundance and delight.

A LIGHTHEARTED LOOK IN THE MIRROR

There's a wise and hilarious picture book about a mother's obsessively good intentions, called *The Seven Silly Eaters*, by Mary Ann Hoberman. The story has to do with food—the particular kind of food that each of this mom's seven children demands each day and that she heroically produces—but if you've ever taken your convictions just the tiniest bit too far, you'll recognize yourself in this story, and you'll laugh. Since it's told in pitch-perfect rhyme and has a delightful surprise ending that has to do with cake, your kids will love it, too.

3

Abundance

In order to become a reader, you've got to have access to books, and the more books you can hold and touch and page through, the better. Literacy programs that work to get books into the hands of kids who might not otherwise get to own them understand this. So do the writers, editors, and librarians who calmly claim that electronic books will never replace the real thing; they know that nothing can beat the look of an illustration on paper, the feel and the sound of turning a page, the particular smell and heft of a bound book.

During their preschool and early elementary school years, I took my kids to the library every other week to scoop up armloads of books like brightly colored fall leaves. The point of our trips wasn't only about getting something good to read at bedtime, it was about feeling like we were getting away with something too good to be true.

There are so few times you can say YES to your child without any hesitation or any limits. You can't do it at snack time or bedtime or on a play date or at the grocery store or the toy store or even at the park, where it's not OK to climb up the slide when someone else wants to slide down and it's not OK to stay when the wind picks up and it begins to get dark. Camping or a day at the beach are two activities that also lend themselves to saying YES—YES, you can dig a bigger hole; YES, we can stand here in the water all day; YES, you can stay up late to look at the stars. But most of us can't camp out or hang out at the beach as often as we'd like. We can, however, go to the library and say YES to books.

The library my girls and I liked the best was a small neighborhood branch of the local public library. It was housed in a cinder-block building at the near end of a large park, where there are tennis and basketball courts, and a playground with some of the last metal play equipment in the city. There is nothing remotely fancy about the children's section of this library—no animal-shaped beanbags, no semicircle of carpeted steps—but the children's librarians know their books and their clientele.

The librarians present new and selected titles for children on an open wooden rack. "New" means recently reviewed in the *New York Times,* read on PBS's *Reading Rainbow,* or just published from such beloved authors as Cynthia Rylant or Gail Carson Levine. "Selected" means books on Martin Luther King Jr.

in January and on California history when the elementary school curriculum turns its focus on Missions and the Gold Rush. After my kids headed for their favorite shelves, I went straight for the rack—with anticipation and anxiety—as if the best books would be torn out of my grasp at the last moment by a mom just a few seconds faster than me. I was always delighted at what was there for me just to *take.*

After gathering children's books, I would sneak away to the shelf where the librarians put their recommended selections for adults. I usually only had about forty seconds to grab a title before one or the other of my kids would notice I had stepped away and start calling, "Mooooom?" across the library, so I learned to work fast. In this way, I took home books I might never have chosen, such as Elizabeth Berg's easy, straightforward fiction and *Piano Lessons,* the moving book about music and motivation by Noah Adams.

My kids picked up on my habits. Even as a toddler, Emily would go for the box of board books and start stacking Helen Oxenbury titles on one of the low, worn benches of the long, wooden tables. She always chose books that featured animals or babies or both. Carlyn zeroed in on series that featured quirky characters or adventure of some kind—the Arthur books, the Nate the Greats, or the Henry and Mudge's—and soon she was able to pinpoint individual titles she liked in the wide expanse of picture books.

The day each child could print her name and get a library card of her own was a milestone, particularly for Emily, who had watched Carlyn using her library card for years before she got her own. We accidentally sailed right past the time when Emily was first eligible. All she had to do was be able to print her own name, and *that* she could do when she was four. But it wasn't until she had turned six that it occurred to us to have her do it.

One afternoon we were on our way to the library to pick out a book for Carlyn's fourth-grade report on a historical figure. In the car, Carlyn realized that her library card would expire that very day.

"I want a library card," Emily said quietly.

There was a moment of silence before Carlyn cried out, "You can get one! Mom! She can get a library card."

"I can?" Emily asked.

Carlyn and I assured her that it was true.

We went immediately to ask the librarian for an application, and I filled in all the necessary information. Emily stood on her tiptoes to write her name on the form, and then she stood back down to wait for the librarian to hand her a card.

"Your card will come in the mail in about a week," the librarian explained, "As soon as you sign your name on the back of the card, you can start checking out books."

Emily flashed her eyes at me, her lips pressed together in disappointment.

Every day after school that week, Emily shoved her backpack into my arms and ran home to see if her library card had arrived in the mail. She couldn't reach the mailbox herself, so she had to wait for me to catch up and then she had to wait for me to shuffle through the bills and the coupons and the letters to see if the card was there, but she still ran full steam ahead down the sidewalk each day, hoping. When the card finally arrived, it came in a very official-looking envelope with the city seal on the front and Emily's name typed out behind the vellum window. She ripped the envelope apart, inspected the card to make sure it had her name on it, then leaped around the kitchen, waving her card in the air and chanting, "Where do I sign? Where do I sign?"

We waited for Carlyn to come home, and then we went immediately to the library, where Emily checked out eleven books. As the librarian placed Emily's selections in a grocery bag from the local market, she kept up a running commentary on each one—"Oh, *We're Going on a Bear Hunt* is one of my favorites," "Hmmmm, you must really like *Henry and Mudge*." Emily stood transfixed while she listened and watched. She insisted on carrying the bag, which had to weigh half as much as she did, to the car herself.

Most of our trips to the library were just like that. On each visit, we would take home fifteen, seventeen, twenty books, and pile them at the end of the girls' beds where they could, almost literally, wallow in them. It didn't make any difference that we would never read them all, that a book on extraterrestrial life was way beyond the kids' understanding, or that every once and awhile one of the books would disappear into thin air (under the bed? behind the dresser?) and I would have to pay the late fee or the replacement cost. What mattered was having the experience of abundance.

BOOKS APLENTY, BOOKS GALORE

One fun way to bring an abundance of books into your kids' lives is to hold regular book exchanges with neighborhood friends. Have your kids set aside all the books on their shelves that they adore. Take the left-overs—the books they've outgrown, the books they don't love—and put them into a box. On the appointed day, everyone brings their box to one friend's house and goes "shopping" among everyone else's castoffs. Any books that are not claimed at the end of the exchange can be donated to a shelter, preschool, or library.

Check with your local librarian for special book sale days, which are usually held once or twice a year. When each book is only a dime or a quarter, you can get bags and bags of books for a few dollars.

A few times a year, abundance comes to us through the Chinaberry book catalog. I love this catalog. I always want to order every single book on its pages. Sometimes, I do the next best thing. I announce that we're going to place a Chinaberry order. We turn down page corners with abandon, circle reviews we like, and pretend that there are no limits. After a few days have passed, we narrow our selections and order three or four books each. They come a few days later like freshly picked fruit delivered straight from the orchard.

4

Delight

It takes a long time to learn how to read. It's a tedious and frustrating process, filled with uninspiring words like *see* and *the* and *bat* and difficult words like *their* and *knife* and *when*. I was best at passing along my love of reading when I seized opportunities to make it fun. These opportunities present themselves all the time, if you're looking. I find that the place they come up most often is in the car, when you're driving from place to place. My girls and I would sing in the car, play word games, quiz each other, make up goofy words and lyrics. As a result, my kids were "marinated" in the skills needed for reading—a description I once read in a *New York Times* editorial from a kindergarten teacher arguing about the benefits of whole-language learning. Whenever I think of this concept—of kids soaking in a rich pool of language, where letter sounds are learned through gameplay and spontaneous rhymes teach key vocabulary—I think of the word *Madagascar.*

The summer before she entered kindergarten, Emily fell in love with the word *Madagascar.* Madagascar is one of those words like *hallelujah, jiffy, Ebenezer Scrooge,* and, *wingdingdilly* that feels good on the tongue and sounds nice to the ear.

I once overheard a dad trying to teach his little girl the word *apple,* which was spelled out on her juice box. They were sitting at a table at one of those giant indoor playground gyms, waiting for their pizza. While I couldn't see them, I could clearly make out their conversation.

"A-a-a," the dad was saying, "pull. Aaaaa-pullll."

The child didn't respond so the dad pressed on.

"See the first letter? That's an *A.* That makes the *A-a* sound."

The child still didn't respond.

At this point, I couldn't squelch my curiosity. I turned in my chair to get a glimpse of the kid who was resisting such intense efforts—and I saw that she was only about two years old. She was a tiny little thing, with flyaway blonde hair, and she was sitting there sipping her apple juice, ignoring her dad.

How much better it would have been for the dad to fill their pizza-waiting time with a few words that were fun to say! To play a little rhyming game with words like *banana* or *butter finger* and to leave the letter-sound drill for a time when his child already loved some words and was begging him to know what the small print on the bottom of the juice box said. Kids love language—the sheer sound of it—and *apple,* as even a two-year-old knows, is a common, dull, and rather dreary word. It pales miserably when placed alongside a fabulous word like *Madagascar.*

Emily first heard *Madagascar* on a television show called *Zoboomafoo,* a clever educational show about all the strange, wild, and wonderful habits of animals from all over the world. The host's mascot was a lemur named Zoboo.

"Zoboo's a lemur," Emily told me as soon as the show was over and we were eating breakfast, "and all lemurs come from Madagascar."

"Really?" I said, although I hadn't listened to what she said. I was looking at the headlines on the newspaper. I was spreading butter on toast.

"Madagascar," she repeated.

"Hmm," I said.

Later that same day, Emily asked me what Madagascar was.

"It's a country," I said, wondering if it was actually a province or a state or a banana republic. "In Africa," I added, for authenticity, although I wasn't even sure that was correct either.

"Madagascar," she said quickly, as if I had just told her that the word means some exotic and exhilarating sporting event or a rare and thrilling emotion.

A few days later, Carlyn and Emily were playing Toy Shop in the family room. Toy Shop is a game in which they buy and sell each other their toys, but it's less about the purchase transaction than it is about deciding which toys are going to be sold. Some days, the shop sells only animals. Other days, it's exclusively books. On occasion, I am given a wallet with some construction paper dollar bills and a handful of plastic coins, and am invited to browse among the rocks and shells on display. I was working in my office at the end of the hall when I heard a yell. My reaction was instinctual: to race to see who was hurt.

"Everyone OK?" I asked.

"We found Madagascar!" Carlyn exclaimed. She was holding the globe, which had recently been for sale. "Look!" Her finger was pointing to an island off the eastern edge of Africa. "It's near Africa!" she said.

"Madagascar!" Emily said, her finger raised as if she'd just made a clever point, "Madagascar!"

I smiled, and got it—the realization dawning on me many days late: Emily *liked* this word. She knew that it meant a specific spot on the map. Zoboo, a creature she adored, lived there. And the word was great fun to say. Whoever said TV wasn't good for kids?

I whipped out a piece of blank paper. "Emily," I said, calling her over, "this is how you write the word *Madagascar.*" I wrote out the word in big letters across the white sheet of paper. I did not capitalize the "M" because I thought it made more sense to have all the letters look the same.

"It's LONG," she said, staring at it. It was, in fact, much longer than *man* and *pan,* which were the only words she'd ever recognized on paper.

"How long is it?" I asked.

"Ten letters," Carlyn said before anyone had time to breathe.

"Carlyn," I said, "let *her.*"

Emily pointed to each letter, counting slowly. "Ten letters," she said. "That's super long!"

"And you know what's cool about it?" I went on. She stared at me like I was talking about Santa Claus. She was prepared to think there was nothing cooler than what I was about to tell her about the word *Madagascar,* and in truth, I'm not sure that, at that moment, there was. "There are a bunch of little words that make it up—words you can *read.*"

Carlyn shouted out, "Mad, gas, car!"

Emily stared at the paper as Carlyn's fingers framed the smaller words.

"Mad-a-gas-car," Emily said, as if she was telling a story. "Mad-a-gas-car. Mad-a-gas-car."

She owned that word, and if it was anything like the words I took to heart when I was a child, Emily would remember it and use it and take delight in it for many, many years to come.

WORD PLAY

The word game my kids and I like best can be done in the car, while cooking dinner, while putting away laundry, or while soaking in the bathtub. It's making up new lyrics to familiar tunes. This game forces you to think on your feet, to understand how rhyme and rhythm works, and it's a great excuse to play around with words. When we really get on a roll, this game turns into a kind of call-and-answer game, where one person sings a verse and the other person adds onto what they've started or makes an argument against the claim that's just been sung. One holiday season, for example, Carlyn and I spent about an hour making up lyrics to "Joy to the World," in which we carried out a mock argument about her clearing her plate from the table: "If you don't clear . . . your plate right now . . . you're going to have to pay!"

Obviously, the whole point of this game is to have fun with words.

5

History

My mom had an innate understanding of the inherent pleasure of words. I have dozens of memories that involve her belief that words are something you acquire and own, like gleaming jewels. Once, my sister was taunting me by calling me a paramecium. She was in seventh grade, and I was in fourth, and I had no idea what she was talking about. Paramecium, however, sounded like the most horrible kind of mean and nasty put-down.

"Mom," I whined, "Laura called me a paramecium!"

My mom's response was cool and clearheaded. "Look it up in the dictionary," she said.

Prompted into action, I found the word in the dictionary and learned that my sister had been calling me an elongated unicellular animal—an easy insult to discount because it was so absurd.

I recall another time when my mom walked into the room where Laura and I were playing. There were LEGOs strewn all over the floor and blocks and little rubber animals. "Pick up all this detritus!" she commanded.

I didn't know, exactly, what *detritus* meant, but I could certainly guess: It was stuff, it was junk, it was things that weren't where they belonged. *Webster's* defines *detritus* as "loose material that results directly from disintegration," but to me it remains a word that carries the contempt of my mom in it—a potent, powerful word that works like no other when the house or the car is a mess.

In addition to collecting words, my mother liked to perform them. She used to read aloud to my dad as he drove across the desert on one of our many trips to the mountains or the rivers of the American West. I recall her reading from the *New York Times Magazine* and *National Geographic*. I would be sitting in the backseat trying to read my *Archie* comic books, but really listening to my mom—not so much to what she was reading as to the sound of her voice as it rose and fell and made specific points. My mom was a reader, and I knew that, without anyone ever having to tell me. I know it still. Whenever she visits me, she brings books that she has read and presses them into my hands with an explanation such as, "My book club had the most lively conversation about this," or, "This is a *wow* book." Whenever I visit her, there will typically be a small stack of books on the windowsill in the room that used to be mine. In this case no words are exchanged. I just know that she has read these books, and that she has left them there because she thinks I will enjoy them. That kind of enthusiasm seeps into your bones.

It seeped in from my dad's side, as well. My dad has read for work and pleasure all his life. He founded the Department of Environmental Studies at the University of California, Santa Barbara, and during his career wrote ten books crammed with ideas and information gleaned from his wide-ranging reading and inspired original thought. His most important work is a textbook called *Wilderness and the American Mind,* which has been used in classrooms for almost forty years and is considered by many to be among the seminal works of wilderness study in this country. The first chapter alone contains references to a book by an eleventh-century Chinese landscape painter, classic Greek mythology, the Bible, a speech by Andrew Jackson, the writings of Abraham Lincoln, the *Saturday Evening Post,* and the novels of Nathaniel Hawthorne, among many other texts—a list that exhibits a huge amount of reading.

One of the results of my dad's devotion to reading is that he really knows how to tell a story. He is brilliant in front of a large class in a lecture hall, spinning stories of early explorers and environmental activists that capture the imagination of thousands of students. I have watched him pin large groups of people around a campfire with tales of his escapades in the wilderness— tales that always seems to involve near-disaster experiences and either a pristine beach, an idyllic hot spring, or a break in the clouds appearing at precisely the perfect moment.

When I was a little girl, my dad made up stories to tell me at bedtime. He would ask me what I wanted the story to be about, and I would pick an animal like a giraffe or a whale. He would give the character some predicament, which may have sprung from his imagination or may have been borrowed from one of the books on our shelf, such as *Paddle to the Sea,* the epic tale of a toy canoe that floats from Lake Superior to the sea, or *The Saga of Pelorus Jack,* the story of an albino dolphin who made it his life's work to steer ships clear of the rocks in Cook Strait, New Zealand. His animal stories were never long, and they never spanned more than one night, but I loved them all the same.

It would be easy to say that I learned a love of reading from my parents and that my children would, then, naturally learn it from me—as if reading were something passed along through the genes, like a pug nose or blue eyes. But the truth is far more complex because there were other activities that my parents felt as passionately about as they did reading, and I did not come to love either of them.

My dad, though he is a scholar, is an adventurer at heart. His scholarship about wilderness stemmed from his passion for being in the wild. We spent an inordinate amount of my childhood on camping, hiking, backpacking, and river trips, and there is no doubt that my sister and I gained the skills to survive and the experience to appreciate the wild. It was hard not to do either with my dad as a guide. But neither my sister nor I came to have any real feeling for the wilderness beyond an intellectual appreciation of it. We both, in fact, live decidedly sedate, suburban lives. We take the occasional ski or river trip with our kids, but we are not out there breaking our fingernails on the cliffs of Yosemite, blistering our hands guiding boats down the Grand Canyon, or chopping wood in a rustic cabin as close to the sound of white water as we can get. My dad reports to us on his continued adventures on the high seas, remote islands, inner gorges, and the mountaintops of the American West; and I listen as if to a citizen from a foreign land that I have never visited. My dad invited us into what he loved, but we didn't stay.

A similar thing happened with my mom and music. My sister and I were made to take piano lessons starting at the age of ten because my mom believed music was the cornerstone of a complete education and a full life. She listened to Puccini operas on the radio as she cleaned the house, played Rodgers and Hammerstein musical scores as she prepared dinner, and belted out the stately hymns in church on Sunday morning as if she were singing in the shower. I played the scales and songs I was asked to play and learned how to read music, but as soon as I was able to convince my mom that I didn't have any talent for the piano, I took up the flute, and quickly after that, a tennis racket. I like to listen to music, and I like the idea of being able to bang out a rousing rendition of "Happy Birthday" or sit down and play "Hark! The Herald Angels Sing" by holiday candlelight, but the practice of music is something that I do not have the patience for.

Once my mother made my sister start playing the piano, however, she never stopped practicing and went on to sing in college glee clubs, earn an advanced degree in music theory, teach music at the university level, and insist that her own children take piano lessons starting at the age of six—bringing the passion for piano playing full circle within one generation.

Children don't miss much. As surely as my sister's kids know that theirs in a house where music is important, mine know that ours is a house where the same is true of books. It's something they identify with in a happy way, and that they go out of their way to profess. For Mother's Day, the year she was in fourth grade, for example, Carlyn brought me a poster of a poem she had made in class. It was one of those projects where you write a descriptive phrase beginning with each letter of a particular word—in this case, "MOTHER." I keep it above my desk, along with Emily's handprints from preschool, and the last card from a dear friend of mine who died. Carlyn's poem goes like this:

> *Most loving*
> *Only mine*
> *The best mom in the world*
> *Her name is Jennie*
> *Everyday she's there for me*
> *loves to Read*

The point is that you can't predict what influences will shape your kids or *how* any given influences will shape them. Your children may be intimately connected to experiences of your passion, but they are, in the end, wholly separate from them. It's the connection, however, that I think is key. It's letting your kids see you doing what you love to do and hearing you express your passion. It's playing with words, playing music, exploring the wide-open wilderness, and seeing what your kids will do with that history, given their particular talents, their particular temperaments, and the passage of time.

CELEBRATE WHERE YOU COME FROM

There's a beautiful picture book by ballerina Libba Moore Gray, which is all about the influence of her mother on her career as a dancer. The mom was not a dancer in any official way. She just loved to move, and she would dance during every season of the year, grabbing her daughter's hands and doing a "leaf-kicking, leg-lifting, hand-clapping, hello-autumn ballet." At the end of the story, the narrator talks about being on stage as a ballerina where she goes "air-daring, leap-flying, wing-soaring," and thinks of her mother who "had a dancing heart and shared that heart with me." The book is called *My Mama Had a Dancing Heart*, and it's a lovely tribute to the role history plays in what we grow up to love.

I also like the book *When I Was Young in the Mountains* by Cynthia Rylant, which captures the pull of having a history in a particular place. The last page of the book says, "When I was young in the mountains, I never wanted to go to the ocean, and I never wanted to go to the desert. I never wanted to go anywhere else in the world, for I was in the mountains. And that was always enough."

6

Talent

Most parents will say that they knew their child had some sort of special characteristic or tendency since the day the child was born. One of my friends, who has four children, believes without a doubt that these traits are as distinct and knowable as green eyes or straight hair. I know a little girl—a friend of Carlyn's and Emily's—who was born with the talent of sympathy. As an infant, this child would crawl over to any other kid who was crying and offer her blanket. As a toddler, she was the first to get a hurt child a Band-Aid. As she grew, her sense of empathy grew along with her to the point where her mom and I are convinced that she will become a nurse or a doctor or some kind of healer.

Carlyn was loud, bold, and verbal from the start, and she was born with an affinity for books. She slept with books the way other kids sleep with teddy bears. At the age of three, she would lie in her bed at night reciting her favorite stories to herself as she went to sleep. Rob and I would go about cleaning up the dinner dishes or reading through the mail to the constant droning babble of memorized words. Sometimes I stood outside the door to Carlyn's bedroom where she couldn't see me, eavesdropping. I would lean against the wall and silently urge her on, struggling to hear which words she got right and which words she invented to make the rhymes work. From the very start, she got the concept that a story is meant to *flow*. Saying these stories to herself, she sounded like she was reading on stage.

One day, just after her little sister Emily was born, three years and three months after her own birthday, Carlyn recited her first book to a public audience—the gathered members of her family who had come to welcome the new baby. She stood up in front of Emily's crib and announced that she was going to read us a book. She handed my mother the book in question—a thirty-two-page picture book by Wong Herbert Yee called *Big Black Bear*—and then she started her performance, reciting the story without making a single mistake as she walked in a small circle around the rug in the middle of the room.

> *Big Black Bear came out from the wood,*
> *Stuck his nose in the air, sniffed something good!*
> *Followed that scent from tree to tree,*
> *Down to the City, where he shouldn't be.*
> *Shuffling along on four furry feet*
> *To a Brown Brick House on Sycamore Street.*

We didn't know that Carlyn had been listening so closely to her bedtime stories. We didn't know that a child's memory can be like a steel trap. We were so stunned that Rob got up, got the camera, and took a snapshot of the performance. In the picture, my mom and dad and I are sitting on the floor exchanging amazed glances as Carlyn paces and recites. There was a tinge of anxiety to our amazement—the way Carlyn was pacing and the precision with which she told this story were slightly troubling in their intensity—but I found the whole thing comfortably familiar. What Carlyn was doing was, in effect, exactly the same thing that I do when I lose myself in a book. Her head was down, her mind was turned inward, and she had given herself over to the sound of someone else's voice.

I was convinced that Carlyn was some sort of reading prodigy, and her very fast and seemingly effortless mastery of reading skills fueled my belief. She went from picking out a few sight words to reading simple chapter books in a few short months, and advanced quickly from there. At age seven, she read *Harry Potter and the Prisoner of Azkaban,* a 732-page book, in twelve days. At age eight, she could flip through twice that many pages in far more complex books, with an uncanny recall of characters and events. When she was nine, she began making sophisticated connections between the books she was reading— jumping up one afternoon, for example, to find the Edward Eager novel *(Seven-Day Magic)* with a character named after the hero of *The Hobbit,* which I was reading her; or telling me at Christmas how the story of Jesus was kind of like the story of Harry Potter because they both featured babies with special powers.

Carlyn's teachers often asked me what I did to spark her intense interest in reading. At first I just joked that reading was in Carlyn's genes, keeping quiet about the way I had hauled away all Carlyn's books when she was two, or how I sometimes insisted on the three-book bedtime story routine even on nights when maintaining routine was counterproductive to everyone's health and happiness. I didn't answer the question honestly because it made me uncomfortable. I wasn't convinced that I had done anything to inspire Carlyn. It was easier to think that she was some sort of genius—until I came across a child who really was.

I met this girl in Carlyn's kindergarten class, where I had eagerly volunteered as a teacher's helper. This is the classic way to support your child's early schooling and a sneaky way to know what's really going on; but with thirty-one kids crammed around the rug, the volunteer's role that year was mostly crowd control. On my first morning, the children had been asked to draw a picture about something they had done over the summer. I moved among the kids at their desks, helping some remember what trips they had taken, exclaiming what a nice job others had done with their stick-figure families, and smiling at Carlyn with pride whenever she glanced in my direction. I came across one girl who had drawn an airplane with a banner unfurled behind it in the sky. Neatly written on the banner were the words "Spirit of St. Louis."

I stopped and blinked at the picture. "Spirit of St. Louis?" I asked, perplexed. I couldn't quite place the importance of the words—Was it the name of an American musical? A battle in the Civil War?—and I couldn't figure out how a five-year-old had managed to comprehend and write them, no matter what they meant. I'd had the same problem when I learned that there was a boy in our neighborhood who had jumped on a two-wheeler when he was just three years old and pedaled off down the street, and I'd had it when I saw a four-year-old girl stand on a stage at a street fair and sing "Tomorrow" with such volume and bravado she could have brought down the house at the Hollywood Bowl. How could a child so young display such incredible mastery?

"I read a book about Charles Lindbergh this summer," the girl explained.

"Oh," I said, remembering now that *Spirit of St. Louis* was the plane Charles Lindbergh flew in the first nonstop solo flight across the Atlantic. I glanced at the girl's paper to see who this genius was, and saw the name Ramona Quimby written neatly in the lower corner. The *Q* was made into a sitting cat, which reminded me—again—of something I couldn't place. I moved on to a desk where someone was struggling over how to draw a house.

"That's nice work, Ramona," I said, before I stepped away.

Carlyn's teacher came up behind me and peered at the paper. "Alexandra," she said to the girl, "please write your real name on your paper. I need to know who did such excellent work."

Then it came to me: Ramona Quimby was a character from a Beverly Clearly novel, which I hadn't read or even thought about since I'd been in the third or fourth grade. Ramona was the little sister of Beezus, the one who, when she finally gets to kindergarten, takes the school by storm. Ramona always drew her Qs as if they were little cats. Alexandra could read as well as

I could; it seemed; and in the first week of school, she was already so bored with the kindergarten curriculum, she was doodling on her work.

My daughter loved books and stories, and she was doing a terrific job learning the skills she needed to become a reader, but she was not a reading prodigy. She was a beautiful, blonde-haired, charming, confident, strong, happy child who loved to run, to eat chocolate, to parade around in her new purple backpack, and to play pet shop with her little sister and I loved her for all I was worth, but she was not a reading prodigy. I knew absolutely nothing about Alexandra's life at home or the thoughts inside her head or the state of her heart, but I wished my child were a reading prodigy, too.

The temptation wasn't so much that I wanted my child to be top dog—although there was certainly some of that mixed into the emotion. The main thing was that I wanted to be excused for caring so much about my kid's success. I wanted a way for her talent to be an act of nature rather than an act of will. The gray line between passion and obsession made me feel a slight sense of shame about our trips to the library and our Madagascar-like word games and the way we recited whole paragraphs from memory at the dinner table. A talent like Alexandra's that had obviously sprung fully formed seemed so much more pure than a talent like Carlyn's that had been coddled, nurtured, and maybe even tricked into fruition.

It wasn't until Carlyn's little sister began to learn how to read and coddling, nurturing, and tricking didn't seem to work that I finally realized that I had, in fact, done something to spark Carlyn's intense love of reading—something any parent could be proud of: I had recognized her gifts, and I had helped her to use and value them.

THE BIRTHDAY JOURNAL

Every year on each of my kid's birthdays, I take a few minutes to sit down and write them a letter in a journal that I keep for just this purpose. I do this, at least in theory, for *them*—so that one day they can read the letters and see what was happening on their birthday and see how they changed from year to year. What always ends up happening, however, is that the exercise turns out to be really useful for *me*. Faced with a blank page of paper and the task of describing what each of my kids is like, I have to really *think* about them. How does she spend her time? What pleases her? What angers her? What does she ask the most questions about? What does she have a flair for? It's a perfect way to recognize a child's unique talents.

I've always wanted to do something similar by keeping a book journal for each child—a list of all the books they read, and their responses to them. It would be such fun to go back in ten, twenty, and thirty years and see what books spoke to them when they were three or thirteen. You'd be able to see the trends and the themes that they gravitated to. I would be able to see how long Emily gravitated toward books with dogs, how many times—really—Carlyn has read Harry Potter, and when they first read the books that they will grow up to say changed their lives.

Somehow, I've never managed to get this project off the

ground, but I haven't completely written it off yet. When I do it, I think I will start a list of all the books I have read as well. I find that unless I own a book, can see it sitting on my bookshelf, touch it, take it out and recommend it to a friend, it becomes harder to hold in my head. Writing down the names of all the books I've checked out of the library or borrowed from friends could be an affordable remedy.

7

Perseverance

Emily is a sweet, observant child who likes puzzles, LEGOs, little stuffed animals, and quiet. She was not born with a love of books. By the time Emily was three, she'd heard *Big Black Bear* read aloud just as many times as Carlyn had, but she never recited it. When she was four, I sat with her, patiently pointing out the words in the short *Paddington Bear* book that was one of the first books Carlyn tried to sound out on her own, and instead of trying to follow my finger and figure out the letter sounds, Emily just said, "Take your hand away, Mom. I can't see the pictures." If I lapsed and accidentally persisted in pointing out the words, she'd get furious, as only a little kid can get furious: "Mooooom! I just want to hear the story!"

Emily sounded out letters, when pressed to do so, silently in her head, and it was a slow and laborious process for her. She easily gave up and dissolved into tears, crying out that it was too hard. She had difficulty pronouncing certain sounds, such as "R" and "SH," and I wondered if the movements of her mouth were mirroring a problem somewhere in the synapses in her brain. Her preschool teachers assured me that they didn't believe this was the case, and a speech specialist concurred that her difficulties with pronunciation were physical limitations she would outgrow. I continued to put my fingers to the words as I read, and I urged her to give some simple words a try; but I did it with more doubt than with Carlyn.

"Emily doesn't memorize stories the way Carlyn did," I said one night to Rob—committing the cardinal sin of parenthood, comparing one child to another.

"She has an amazing memory," Rob reminded me. "Just ask her to tell you which turns to take to get to the movie theater. Or ask her what we did a year ago on July fourth."

"I know, but she doesn't have a memory for *words.*"

"And . . . ?"

"It just bugs me," I mumbled, too ashamed to voice what one of my friends calls "catastrophizing"—the impulse to turn the tiniest aberration in our children's progress into a future catastrophe. The kid's feet turn in? She'll never walk. She stutters? She'll never speak in public. She's got pudgy thighs? She'll be fighting fat forever. My secret fear was that if Emily didn't memorize books, she might not recite them, and if she didn't recite them, she might not easily read them; and if reading wasn't easy, its pleasures and promise would be lost to her forever.

The fact was that Emily's interests and talents lay elsewhere. I learned this one night when we were playing a board game called Labyrinth. It was brand new to us, a recommendation from my sister. It's an ingenious setup, where players try to reach treasures on an ever-shifting board. The only way you can win is to picture the way the maze will look two, three, or four steps ahead.

The age recommendation on the box reads eight and up, but the first time we played, we let Emily give it a try. She was five, so instead of locating her treasure in the order dealt to her, we allowed her to locate her seven treasures at random, but that was the only concession we made to her.

Silently Emily planned and plotted and made the maze open up as if at her command. In several swift moves, toward the end of the game, she gleefully beat us all.

Carlyn, who is often a sore loser, sat back from the board. "Whoa," she said, "that was amazing."

"She was counting cards," Rob said, in a stunned voice. His mother had been a card-counting pro and a bridge-playing champion.

"I knew the last card was the beetle," Emily explained, "because all the other treasure cards were out."

Later, Rob and I discussed Emily's grasp of logic, and we predicted, with private pride, how our five-year-old might grow up to be an engineer or a computer programmer or an architect. But an engineer has to be able to read a report. A computer programmer may want to read about a dot-com millionaire's rise to fame. An architect might get her best inspiration from nineteenth-century English novels. Emily would still have to learn how to read.

I put all my hopes for her reading future into The Big Book, which had done such a great job of preparing Carlyn to read. The Big Book was about two feet by three feet of laminated words and pictures, which the teachers at our neighborhood preschool used to teach the kids about reading. The goal for these four-and-a-half-year-olds wasn't reading itself, but reading readiness, which means that the kids know that letters make sounds and sounds make words, that we read from left to right, that we start at the top and read to the bottom, that we turn a page when there are no more words, and that when we're reading, we're not chewing on our hair or throwing pieces of colored macaroni across the room. The kids looked at The Big Book every day for about ten minutes out of their three-hour program. It was a simple activity, but over time it worked wonders.

For the first two months of the prereading program, Emily refused to even talk about it.

"What was in The Big Book today?" I'd ask her at dinnertime, just as I asked her sister, Carlyn, what had happened on the third-grade playground, and her dad, Rob, what had happened at the office.

"I forget," Emily always answered. She'd invariably say these words with a sly smile—a pressing together of lips, a quick lowering of her eyes. I'd attempt to draw the information out of her, but she'd just repeat the phrase, with increasing annoyance at our questions: I forget, I forget! *I told you I forget!*

I didn't believe her for a second. She has a tiny telltale dimple that appears near her nose whenever she's fibbing or fooling, as if she literally can't keep a straight face. Emily hadn't forgotten what she did at school that day; she just didn't want to say. It was her attempt to grab power in an energetic family of four—just like not wanting to go to bed at bedtime or not wanting to eat the spaghetti if there was too much sauce or not enough cheese.

"Ask her right after school, right when you pick her up," Carlyn suggested. Carlyn is the kind of kid whom you can't get to *stop* talking, so she has a certain authority in matters of getting people to speak up.

"OK," I agreed. The next day when I picked up Emily at noon, I asked her what had been in The Big Book before I said a word about lunch or the painting she held in her hand or whether Lindsay could come over to play.

"I forget," she said.

Soon after Emily's fifth birthday in February, we sat down to eat red pepper pasta—her all-time favorite meal—and she said, "I read the word *man* today."

"*Man?*" I asked.

"*Man?*" Rob repeated.

"And *tan* and *pan*," Emily said, "and *tin* and *pin*."

I swallowed. "Really?" I squealed, feeling elated, as if she had told me she'd learned to fly. I can remember these words—the first she read—far better than the first words she spoke.

Emily smiled, knowing that she had succeeded in pulling off a major surprise.

Carlyn had, by this time, leapt up, grabbed a piece of blank paper and a pen, and raced back to the table. She shoved aside Rob's napkin and wrote out the words *man, pan, tan*.

Emily glibly tapped each word on the page with her finger and read, "*man, pan, tan*."

Rob snatched up the pen and wrote, *tin, pin, win,* and Emily tapped these words and read all of them as well.

"You're reading!" we all cried—even though we knew she was a long way from being able to pick up a book and follow a story line. But she was recognizing words; it was her first giant step, and it deserved a celebration.

I felt cheered by Emily's breakthrough and took it as a sign that she was on track for reading success, until two months later when I showed up in the cafeteria at Seaside Elementary School, along with fifty other preschool parents, to enroll Emily in kindergarten for the following September. We were listening to the principal outline basic philosophies and rules, and I was doodling in the margins of the brightly colored handouts because I'd read the same sheets three years ago when I sat in the same cafeteria to enroll Carlyn. I'd heard it all before—the plea for parents to help out in the classroom, the lunch ticket drill, the hepatitis update—but then the principal was talking about reading, which was something I hadn't heard before, so I looked up to listen.

"Some of those children who just walked out the door are already reading," she said, speaking of all the kids who had paraded out, nervous and curious, to meet their future kindergarten teachers. I looked toward the door as if I would see the readers lined up there, in special formation, making themselves known. It would be a stretch to place Emily among them—a stretch I remembered confidently and naively making with Carlyn before I met the girl who called herself Ramona. Emily may have been able to spell her name, identify big *E*s in the newspaper, and read a handful of simple three-letter words, but no one could honestly classify her as a reader—not even me.

"Some of those kids won't read until the first grade and some of them won't read until the second," the principal cautioned, "and this is OK. Do you hear what I'm saying? It's OK." There was silence in the cafeteria. She had our attention. Not any of the parents in that room wanted their child to be one of the slow ones. "Our goal," she went on, "which is mandated by the state of California, is for all children to be reading—*well*—by the end of the third grade. Now I guarantee you," she said, "that some of you are going to come into my office next January and wonder why your child isn't reading. I'm going to say the same thing I'm saying right now. Kids walk at different ages and they talk at different ages and they read at different ages."

Third grade, I thought incredulously, *third grade?* That was far too long to wait.

I went directly to Borders to look for tools to help me jump-start Emily's reading and ran smack into a flashy stand-alone display of books for beginning readers. It was a new series of learn-to-read books from Candlewick Press. Four slim, staple-bound paperbacks, all written around one theme, huddled together in a thick, shiny outer envelope. I grabbed a set called *Here Comes Tabby Cat*. Each of the four books offered a fully developed little story told in simple words with characters adorably drawn in a bright, simple cartoon style. The text sang with a pleasing rhythm, and the ending of each book surprised the reader with a moment of delight. If Emily could read words in The Big Book at preschool, I was sure she could read the words in the four short volumes of *Here Comes Tabby Cat*.

"These are books you can read," I told Emily, when I presented them to her at bedtime.

"I don't want to read," she insisted. "I want you to read to me."

"I'm going to read them first," I said, "then later, you can read them to me."

I tried to get her to jump in and supply the word *Tabby* at the start of each line I read, by pausing and sort of nodding my head in her direction.

"I caaaaaaaaan't," she wailed. She buried her face in her hands in utter despair.

"You just say *Tabby* each time," I explained.

"I want you to just read it, Mom," she whined.

"Fine," I said, and put my finger up to the first word to begin the next line.

"No fingers, Mom," she pleaded.

After about a week, she grudgingly consented to participating. I showed her how all the books were about a cat named Tabby and how all the words were small. I read through the title called *Cat Bath,* and then I read it again.

> *Tabby Cat washes her paw.*
> *Tabby Cat washes her ear.*
> *Tabby Cat washes her nose.*
> *Tabby Cat washes her leg.*
> *Tabby Cat washes her back.*
> *Tabby Cat washes her tail.*
> *Now Tabby Cat is all clean.*
> *So Tabby Cat washes Sammy.*

"Now you try it," I said, handing over the book. It had a pleasing heft to it, an enticing gloss. She took it.

She pointed to each word, as I had done, and read the story, slowly, pronouncing each word as if it stood on its own. She didn't quite get it right. On the second-to-last page, when the repeated phrase changed, she missed the word "Now" and stumbled at the word "clean" because she couldn't remember what it was or how it sounded, but she got the *idea* of reading a story as she never had before.

"Rob! Carlyn!" I yelled. "Come quick!"

They came and piled on Emily's bed beside us, and Emily made her way through the story again, stumbling on the same words she had a moment before. When she was done, Carlyn said, "Um, that was good, Emily, but when you *really* know how to re——"

"Carlyn, stop!" Rob shouted.

"What?" she said, in her eight-year-old know-it-all voice. "She's not really re——"

"Carlyn!"

"OK!" she protested, wondering why we were making such a big fuss when Emily's success was due, in such large part, to her memorizing a pattern. What Carlyn didn't remember was that we had fussed just the same way over her doing just the same thing at just the same age, and that the fussing was a potent form of confidence building.

I left the Tabby Cat books by Emily's bed. She didn't touch them for ten days, and on every single one of those afternoons, she complained to me about being bored and having nothing to do. Some days I would suggest that she set up a zoo or make a bead necklace. Other days I would invite her to cook with me— pizza dough or lentil soup or peanut butter cookies. Still other days, I'd lecture her that it's not the mom's job to entertain her kids twenty-four hours a day. One day, when I was trying to get some work done before dinner, I said, "Have you read the Tabby Cat books? That's something you could do."

"I don't know how to read," she said. Her shoulders drooped from her small frame. Her wispy blonde hair hung forlornly over her eyes.

"That's not true!" I cried, "You can look at the pictures and tell yourself the story, and I know you can get some of the words right because I've heard you do it."

"I don't want to," she said. "I hate being five! It's so boring! There's nothing to do, and you're being so mean to me!"

I took her in my arms and tried to soothe her troubled spirits, confident that everything would be better when she was able to pick up a book, sink into a chair, and lose herself in a story.

SOAK UP THE PLEASURES OF THE BOOKSTORE

Perseverance is a whole lot more fun when there are goals and incentives. The thing with reading is that you have a natural, built-in reward system—and it has nothing to do with sugar. Take every opportunity you can to reward your child with a trip to the bookstore. Most books for kids who are learning to read are under five dollars, which makes it relatively easy to indulge; and being in the bookstore itself, with license to spend, is a thrill. As James Carroll, the *Boston Globe* columnist, wrote, "Bookstores are bustling, lively places. Large and small, in cities and suburbs, at night or in midmorning, they are a joy to enter, with staff who actually seem to love what they do; with stock displayed to excite the gaze; with customers entirely unlike customers in other kinds of stores. . . . The book is the best thing human beings have done yet: and in the booming bookstores of America, it has found an accidental shrine."

Go to the shrine. Soak up the pleasures. And offer them to your child as well.

If you feel overwhelmed by the vast number of choices at the bookstore, start keeping a "What to Read" file. Whenever I hear of a good book or see a great review or hear an interesting author interview on the radio, I write the name of the book down and throw it in this file. When it's time to go to the bookstore, the file comes with me.

While you wait to build up your file, or if it's a little thin, go to one of the many book-related Web sites on the Internet and get some inspiration. Here are a few places that I find really easy and helpful:

1. www.kidsread.com: This is a site run by the folks at www.BookReview.com, and they know their books. You can read reviews on this site, check out the featured books, go to the "We Asked, You Said" area to see what kids are saying about popular books, and write to authors.
2. www.carolhurst.com: Carol Hurst is a long-time children's book professional, and her site is packed with extremely useful information about books and reading. You can search for books by grade or by theme, among many other things.

3. www.cbcbooks.org: This is the site of the Children's Book Council (CBC). They've got author interviews, a "Hot Off the Press" section for just-released books, a "Bimonthly Showcase" of books by topic, and an "Awards & Prizes" page.

4. The American Library Association at www.ala.org: There is a wealth of book-related information on this site, including the top one hundred libraries list and lists especially for reluctant readers. Click on the button labeled "Kids, Parents, and The Public."

5. www.greatbooks.org: The Great Books Foundation is a program designed to bring great books into the schools through parent-reader volunteers. The books they use are listed by age and grade, which makes it easy to search.

8

Arrogance

My arrogance about reading did not only apply to the belief that my children would learn to read and learn to love it, but to *what* they would read as well. Throughout first grade, all Carlyn brought home from the school library were large-format-picture-book rewrites of Disney's bestselling movies. Week after week on library day, she'd haul home lifeless versions of *Sleeping Beauty* or *The Little Mermaid*. She didn't want to tackle these books on her own—mastering her understanding of phonics, wrestling with the words she didn't know, and stretching her reading muscles. The idea was that *I* should read them as soon as she got home from school, just before dinner, just after dinner, and at bedtime. They took at least a half hour to slog through, and there wasn't a single turn of phrase in them that sang. I found myself reading the words with no feeling, as if I were reading a tax return.

I finally cracked and approached her teacher, Mrs. Murphy, one day when I went to pick Carlyn up from school.

"Can you help me out," I asked, "with Carlyn's choices at the library?"

"She sure loves those Disney books," Mrs. Murphy said.

"I know, and I can't take it anymore."

Mrs. Murphy looked at me and smiled—a perfectly lovely, patient, teacherly smile. "Don't worry," Mrs. Murphy explained, "she'll outgrow them soon enough."

"I certainly hope so," I said—and then I thought about it for a long, long time. *She loves them.* That was the thing I wanted.

Hadn't I loved *Archie* comic books? My sister and I would stuff them in the backseat for long car rides across the mountains and the desert, wanting to be Veronica, certain that we were, in fact, Betty. And I loved *Teen* magazine. My favorite issues were the back-to-school issues. Since I had short, curly brown hair, I poured over the makeovers of girls with sleek, long hair and studied the fashion spreads of students on leaf-studded paths in front of brick buildings. I was a California girl who did my learning in a town where the leaves never change, but I read every word of the stories about creating a fall wardrobe and fixing a sleek hairdo.

Soon enough the teen drama ceased to be of interest, and I began to read books with more substance. I read adventure stories starring the plucky Caddie Woodlawn, and I dreamed of haylofts and walking the dusty road to school in the company of brothers I didn't have. I read *Riders of the Pony Express,* loving the words that described the land and the dangers. These were things I knew of from my travels with my family—the red rock canyons of the West, the threat of twisted ankles. At some point during junior high, I discovered Miles Franklin's Australian memoir, *My Brilliant Career,* and knew that one day I, too, would fill a ream of blank white paper with words.

"How did you get me to stop reading trashy books when I was a kid?" I asked my mom. I often argue with my mom over my children's eating habits, their manners, and their busy schedules; but she's such a dedicated, serious, and enthusiastic reader, and I thought that she would have some clever advice that could help me improve Carlyn's library selections.

"We didn't worry so much about things like that," she said.

I decided to pretend that my mom and Mrs. Murphy were right, and I dutifully read the Disney books, but I didn't really believe that it was contributing to anything worthwhile. It would take me three years of repeatedly making the same assumption before I finally took the lesson to heart in a white room in the pediatric wing of my local hospital.

My epiphany came late one summer day when Emily was five. She had been playing with a friend and climbing on the footboard of her bed when she slipped, fell, and snapped both the bones in her forearm. When I heard the shriek, I sped into her room to find her wrist and hand hanging at a grotesque angle and the color draining out of her face.

"I can't move my arm," she whispered.

"OK," I said, trying to collect myself, "OK." I scooped her up and raced to the phone, then decided calling anyone was a waste of time. I raced to the car, then sped back inside because I'd forgotten my purse. I paused at the phone again, didn't call anyone, then sped back to the car. I was worried that Emily was going to pass out. I was worried that her friend would be stuck with me at the emergency room for the next seven hours. I was worried that once I arrived at the hospital, the authorities would take Emily away from me and declare me an unfit mother because this was the second time in two years she'd broken an arm by falling from a piece of furniture.

I got my neighbor to take the friend home and drove to the urgent care facility at our family doctor's office, shouting at Emily, who was in her car seat in the backseat, to keep her from passing out: "Don't close your eyes, Emily! Breathe, Emily! BREATHE." I was so focused on Emily's clammy-looking skin and rolling eyes that I don't recall looking at the road, the other cars, or any of the stoplights we passed. I chose my family doctor's office over the emergency room because they knew I wasn't a bad mother and they allowed Emily to fall asleep in my lap while they x-rayed her arm. I held her hot and broken body until Rob met us at the orthopedic surgeon's office an hour later, and then we all drove together to the hospital to prepare for the surgery that would wrench Emily's arm back into place.

Before the surgery to set her arm, Emily had to have blood tests and needle pricks; there were nurses with instructions about not eating, and doctors whose faces did nothing but frown.

"I'm just like Curious George," Emily announced.

I never liked *Curious George*. Like the Disney picture books, I balked at reading them. It's not that I wanted my kids to read only award-winning, time-honored books of confirmed cultural merit—as if there's even an agreement as to which books fall into these categories—it's that I wanted them to at least read books that had some meat, some teeth, some heart. A picture book like Ian Falconer's *Olivia* has cleverness and visual sophistication and a hilarious protagonist pig. A chapter book like *Mr. Putter and Tabby Pick the Pears* conveys messages about being a good neighbor, accepting the cranky knees you may get when you grow older, and making good use of the eccentric gifts you get from people you love. But *Curious George* has always seemed to me like a celebration of bad behavior.

It's true that Curious George is himself an adorable monkey with a keen sense of adventure, who performs a lot of antics to hold a child's attention. But George gets away with everything just short of murder. He lies, he cheats, he steals, he defaces property—and all he has to do is smile, and not only is everything forgiven by the man with the yellow hat, but he's offered starring roles in movies and the chance to fly to the moon. I could not bring myself to read the stories without making social commentaries, so Rob became the reader of *Curious George* in our house, first with Carlyn and later with Emily. When I was in a generous mood, I opened the big yellow book of *Curious George* stories and slogged through one of them, adding my own snide editorial remarks about appropriate behavior and the law of natural consequences.

As soon as Emily evoked the name of Curious George in the hospital, I remembered that George had been to the hospital not once, but twice: the first time when he swallowed a piece of a jigsaw puzzle, the second time when he broke his leg jumping off a fire escape. George had had his blood drawn. George had been put to sleep with a medicine that came from a mask. George had gotten a cast. George was our savior.

"Right!" I exclaimed. "And remember how he sniffed that funny gas and fell asleep, and they had to put him in a shower to wake him up? That's what's going to happen to you, except we're not going to put you in a shower."

Emily nodded.

"And remember how happy George was when his surgery was over and he got to eat ice cream and take the puzzle piece home? That's how you're going to feel, except you're not going to get a puzzle piece. And you're definitely not going to go whizzing down the hall on the food cart."

Emily softened and smiled. Thanks to *Curious George,* we were no longer in uncharted territory.

THE THREE-CHAPTER RULE

I've devised an effective way to combat my tendency to rush to judgment about what my kids are reading, and it has spilled over into the reading I do for myself, as well. I call it the three-chapter rule. All it means is that you give any book three chapters before you decide that you don't like it. (In the case of a picture book, I read the whole book three times.) This prevents you from, literally, judging a book by its cover or by its reputation or by one single element that you can't stomach. It also means that if you suggest a book to your child, she can't dismiss it out of hand. Together, my kids and I have decided not to read *The Phantom Tollbooth* (which I loved as a child, but which I think was too advanced when we tried it), *On the Banks of Plum Creek*, and *Alice in Wonderland*, even though we got more than three chapters into that. But together we tried—and loved—the original version of *Peter Pan*, *The Wheel on the School*, and *Ella Enchanted*. Now when I tell the kids that I'd really rather not read something, they know that I'm not just being rash; I have given it a reasonable chance.

9

Vision

I used to beg to be allowed to do my homework in my dad's study while he worked at his Olivetti typewriter. It hummed when he turned it on, and it had green keys that made a distinct and pleasant click as his hands flew over them. I didn't know what he was writing at the time, but I knew that they were words and that he was making them up as he went along and that if I was quiet, I could stay with him in the study while he wrote. I would stay, with my breath held, to do my homework, doodle, or read. I loved the idea that you could sit alone in a room that was quiet and write words that someone else, in some other time and place, could pick up and read and understand. I stayed in the study to be part of that process, and as I witnessed it, I developed a picture—a vibrant, Technicolor vision—of myself as a writer, too.

Now that I'm a parent, I'm keenly aware of what a fragile business it is to decide what you are going to be or what you are going to do. It seems that the decision hangs on just a few key moments, teeters there in the balance just waiting for someone to say, "But of course you could be president," or, "They just may fly to Mars in your lifetime," or, "You're very good at drawing animals." Kids get asked all the time what they want to be when they grow up, and it's amazing to me that they always have an answer. Whenever I can, I try to encourage whatever they say.

Kindergarten is a big year for thinking about what you want to be when you grow up. One Friday just after Halloween, Emily brought home a shoebox decorated with magazine photos and stuffed with books she'd made in school. "This is my book box," she announced, clutching it to her chest as if it was full of treasure. "I can read all the books inside." She gave me a typewritten note from Mrs. Murphy, who had moved from first grade to kindergarten just in time to teach Emily:

This is my book box. I will keep it in a special place.
These are books I can read by myself. I should read them
every day so I can be a great reader.

"This is so cool!" I said, thinking that Mrs. Murphy was a genius, "What's inside?"

"I'll show you," Emily said. She sat at the kitchen table and fished out a 5 × 7-inch book, stapled together and colored with crayon. "This one is about pumpkins."

"Pumpkins by the haystack, pumpkins by the barn," she

read. "Pumpkins by the porch, pumpkins by the pond." She was pointing at each word as she read, and she moved through them with a new speed and confidence. I sat across from her, savoring the moment.

She fished out another book, called "I Can Be." On each page was a different statement of future potential: "I can be a cook," "I can be a doctor," "I can be a dancer." The last page had been left blank for the kids to draw in their own vision. Emily had drawn a picture of herself—a yellow-haired girl in a red dress, sitting at a table. "I can be a writer," was the text she wrote underneath, obviously with some adult's help.

"A writer!" I said, when she read the final page. "Just like me?"

"I'm going to be a mom and a writer," she said, "just like you."

"Those are good things to be," I said. "What did some of the other kids want to be when they grow up?"

"Tons of kids said soccer player," she reported, "and veterinarian. Lots of the boys said fireman."

I nodded, wondering if there was anyone in Emily's class who would, in fact, grow up to be the things they stated when they were six years old. "Well, you're certainly going to be a reader when you grow up," I said, by way of congratulations. "I can't believe you can read all the books in this box!"

Emily squinted at me like she was trying to get a joke. "A reader?" she asked.

"Well, yeah," I explained, confused by her confusion, "you'll be a reader when you grow up. You're a reader *now!*"

"There's no such thing as a reader, Mom," Emily said

"If you read, you're a reader."

"But you can't *be* that," she repeated, "A reader is just someone who . . ." she paused, sorting out her thoughts, "likes to read!"

I knew what she meant. There's something about reading that's not entirely legitimate. You don't win trophies or tournaments for being a reader. Being a reader sometimes feels like it doesn't even *count*. One afternoon when she was in fourth grade, Carlyn said to me, without preamble, "Sometimes I feel really out of place."

"At school?" I asked, since we were there at the time. It was late in the afternoon, and we had come back to school so she could have the monkey bars and the swings to herself.

"Yeah," she said. "I don't like tetherball or soccer, and I can't play handball. I stink at it. The only things I'm good at are reading, writing, and drawing."

"Those aren't things that make you feel like you have a place on the playground, are they?"

She shook her head. It was clear that being good at handball would, at that moment, have been preferable to being good at reading. I could have launched into a practical discussion of the ways that reading could be put to use in the real world—but that wasn't the point. The skills that are considered valuable on the playground, and often in life, are the skills that can be performed or put to clear and immediate use. Reading is usually valuable only to the person who enjoys it. Carlyn already knew this, and as Emily's comment about not being able to be a reader when you grow up proved, Emily was beginning to sense it.

"But the note from Mrs. Murphy," I said to Emily, "talks

about becoming a great reader. You can grow up to be a mom and a writer, and you can also be a reader. You can grow up to be *anything* and also be a reader."

I got the feeling Emily didn't buy it. She hadn't yet formed a vision of herself as a reader, or anything else for that matter. She was still identifying with who I was and what I did, but that was a solid place to start.

"Mrs. Murphy told us to keep our box somewhere special," she said, ignoring me. She took her book box and stashed it underneath her bed alongside her other prized possessions—the small ceramic animals she'd painted at the clay store, a miniature Fiesta tea set, and the plastic bin of Beanie Babies—and then she came back out and asked if she could watch TV.

Near the very end of her year in kindergarten, Emily was fussing so much at her bedtime that, out of desperation, I told her she could leave her light on for fifteen minutes after we said good night to her, and she could read just like Carlyn did every night. I don't know why I hadn't thought of this earlier, because now, instead of calling constantly for water, or to be tucked in again, or for a stuffed animal she couldn't find, Emily just quietly looked at books until we came in and told her it was time to turn off her light.

Not long after we started this new routine, Carlyn had a friend over to watch a big Laker basketball game, and during one of the commercials, Carlyn and Tessa started talking about *Anne of Green Gables*. Tessa was telling Carlyn how much Carlyn was like Anne in the way she would never stop talking and had "a scope for imagination."

As they were laughing over this comparison, Emily piped in, in a voice that was just aching to be big. "I've been reading a great book," she said smugly.

The older girls stopped, and allowed Emily room to speak.

"It's an early reader," Emily said.

"Good for you," Tessa said cheerfully.

Emily had, in her own mind anyway, become a reader.

THE REASONS FOR READING

What's the point of reading? While your kids are learning, they may wonder, and it's up to you to answer. There are, of course, a million different reasons to read. To help my kids wrap their arms around some of the best ones, I wrote a story called *The Reasons for Reading*. You can download it at www.jennienash.com, or type it out with each line on a separate sheet of paper and let your child color pictures to go along with the text. Try adding some examples of your own.

The Reasons for Reading

Just as the sun comes up in the morning, the baker reads chocolate chip cookie recipes to find the one that uses the most chocolate chips.

Late at night the student reads a textbook to learn if George Washington really had wooden teeth.

During her lunch hour, the doctor reads a mystery about a miracle cure that comes from a tropical plant.

As the siren rings through the city streets, the fireman reads the street signs so he can get to the fire at the forest's edge.

While waiting for the elevator, the scientist reads a journal to learn what other scientists have discovered about the moon and the stars.

As soon as he gets home at the end of the day, the banker reads the newspaper so he can know when his favorite musician is coming to town to play.

As he rides an airplane to play in the World Series, the baseball player reads a novel about the man who hit the longest home run in history.

The artist looks at beautiful pictures in magazines because they remind her of beautiful pictures she's seen at the museum.

The mother reads to her child every night at bedtime because it feels so good to sit together, spin a story, and let the sounds of the words fill the air.

10

Faith

I have a good friend whose youngest child couldn't crack the reading code. Every time he looked at a letter, he agonized over what its name was and what its sound was and how those sounds fit together. The mom went to the library just like I did and spent countless hours reading to her kid just like I did, but nothing seemed to help. In second grade, the mom had the boy tested to see if he had a vision problem or dyslexia, and when those tests came back negative, she tried special tutors and special programs. It really wasn't until third grade that it became clear that this boy would read, and despite a calm assurance from the principal that this was within the normal developmental range, it was an agonizingly long time for his parents to wait. What got them through was love, patience, and faith—

faith that one day all the pieces of the puzzle would fall into place and their son would master this skill.

I saw that kind of faith work wonders for one would-be-reader in Emily's kindergarten class. This girl had Down's syndrome. Her name was Emily, too, and they called her Emily E. The policy in our school district is to mainstream special needs children into a regular kindergarten class with a dedicated adult helper to guide them through the day. The kids in the class became very attached to Emily E. Despite the fact that she looked different from the other students, walked differently, talked differently, and was governed by a different set of more lenient rules, the kids innately understood that she was part of their society and that if she did well, they all benefited. Mrs. Murphy, their amazing teacher, enhanced this understanding by letting Emily E. put extra marbles in the marble jar whenever she sat still or listened or accomplished a small task. When I came to school to help out in the classroom on Wednesday mornings, I often saw the girls trying to help Emily E. stay in the recess line or sit on her spot on the rug. They learned how to touch her shoulders and guide her where she needed to be because the more marbles in the jar, the more rewards the class could earn—be it a popcorn party, a trip to the treasure box, or an extra story.

Over time, the effort to include Emily E. in the society of the classroom blossomed into true affection. In February, the month my Emily turned six, we had a birthday party at our house with all the girls from the class. It was a pajama party. Emily E. was late to arrive, and for the forty-five minutes while they waited for her to come, the other girls kept asking, "Where's Emily E.?

Where's Emily E.?" She finally arrived at our curb, and all seven kindergarteners bolted from the house to greet her and stood on the sidewalk, in the dark, in their pajamas, jumping up and down as she got out of the car. They ushered her into the house to get her settled inside, to get her a piece of a pizza and a cup of orange soda. Emily E. watched them playing their games, happy to be among her friends, and the girls continually stopped to check to make sure Emily E. had what she needed.

I never gave much thought to how Emily E. was doing academically. I assumed that the point of kindergarten for a child like Emily E. was socialization. I should have known better because I'd made that precise mistake before with a friend from church whose son has cerebral palsy. Marianne had been telling me that she and her husband were disappointed that Charlie had been rejected from being mainstreamed in kindergarten, and we were talking about the special school where he would enroll.

"What are the goals for the kids at the school?" I asked. My friend looked at me in an odd way and answered that their goals for Charlie were exactly the same as ours for my kids—that they grow up to be happy, self-aware, self-sufficient members of society.

One day when I was helping in Emily's class with a writing project about safety rules, I happened to notice Emily E. sitting at the back kidney-bean-shaped table with her helper, Mrs. Yang. This is where they usually sat, but I'd never much noticed what they did there. What I saw was Emily E. slapping Mrs. Yang's hand off the letter Mrs. Yang was trying to get Emily E. to read. They were large letters, and they spelled a short sentence. Mrs. Yang was pointing to each letter, asking Emily E. to sound it out. Emily E. wanted to do it on her own, so she was pushing Mrs. Yang's hand away. She couldn't do it on her own, however, so student and teacher were locked in a struggle.

I was mesmerized. This was an exact replay of the scene my Emily and I had had night after night over bedtime stories. This seemed to be a universal struggle with kids learning to read—the fight to take control, to make the connection between what was on the page and what was formed in the mouth.

A few weeks after witnessing this scene, I was walking home from school with my Emily and her friend Samantha.

"Emily E. read to the class today!" Emily told me.

"She was *good*," Samantha added.

"She was better than Michael!" Emily exclaimed.

"What did she read?" I asked.

"A book called *I Can See*," Samantha told me.

"She was loud and clear and she showed all the pictures," Emily said.

I probed the girls more about Emily E's reading demonstration and learned that she had been so happy with her effort, she'd given Mrs. Yang a hug and clapped for her own performance. She'd pressed her hand to her mouth and giggled, the way I sometimes see people do when they've been presented with an award they didn't expect to win.

Emily E's parents, teachers, and friends all believed that she could be a reader, and it seemed, at that moment, that belief was all anyone needed. Perhaps reading was less a learned skill than a natural outgrowth of faith.

TOOLS FOR RELUCTANT READERS

Read-aloud experts have reams of evidence to support the importance of reading aloud to all children, but especially to children who are reluctant readers or who have special needs. Jim Trelease, author of *The Read-Aloud Handbook* and the acknowledged guru on the topic, discusses some of this evidence on his Web site, www.trelease-on-reading.com. This site is a rich resource full of fabulous facts, inspiring stories, and terrific reading lists for reading aloud to kids of all ages and abilities.

Another great tool for kids who are struggling with reading are Language Wrap-Ups. These cool, plastic, key-shaped wraps let kids learn simple words by using their eyes and their hands. You hold the wrap in one hand (it looks a little bit like a ruler), and wrap a string from notch to notch with the other, matching words with meanings. There are sets for letters, letter sounds, sight words, compound words, synonyms, homonyms, and more. Each set features about 240 words and costs about eight dollars at www.learningwrapups.com. My kids mastered their basic math facts using Math Wrap-Ups, challenging themselves to do each wrap in a minute, then in thirty seconds, and finally twenty. The language sets were added too late for us to enjoy, but we've just ordered the new Pre-Algebra set and a beginning Spanish set.

11

Individuality

There are so few times as a parent when anyone congratulates you for your effort. Most of the time, in fact, you're quite unclear about your progress. I have a friend who says parents are "all just nervous and proud and neurotic and unsure." I have another friend who recently went through a lunch box crisis that perfectly illustrates the point. This dad was home after a long business trip and had taken the morning off to help the kids get ready for school. He'd made his famous roast beef and took special care to slice it thin for a sandwich for his fifth-grade son. He carefully wrapped the sandwich in tin foil and packed it in his son's lunch box. But when the boy came home at the end of the day, and the dad asked how he'd liked the sandwich, the boy said, "I'm sorry, Dad. I couldn't eat it."

"Why not?" the dad asked, confused and hurt by this revelation.

"You wrapped it in tin foil."

"Tin foil," the dad repeated flatly.

"The dorky kids wrap their sandwiches in tin foil, Dad. I threw it out."

The parent-teacher conference is the one place where you can hope to be redeemed. It's built into the system. The odds of your child succeeding or even *excelling* at something on the long list of skills and requirements is good, and it's the teacher's job to tell you all about it. Best of all, the teacher is not your friend—not, in other words, someone whose existence depends on making you feel good about your parenting efforts. "Johnny has superb citizenship," the teacher might say, or "Sally's math skills have improved dramatically." These are not, of course, actual commentaries on how you're doing as a parent, but they're taken that way. It's so hard to do otherwise. Unless there is strong evidence to the contrary, society assumes that a bad child is the fault of the parent's misguided efforts, and a good child is the result of the parent's successful efforts. Maybe we want parents to be godlike because it's too painful to consider the alternative—which is that we have no control at all.

I couldn't wait for Emily's first parent-teacher conference. I was hoping that Mrs. Murphy would extol Emily's amazing virtues as a student and a person. After all, I'd seen Emily's neatly written sentences; I went to the classroom on the day she read *The Berenstain Bear's Big Bear, Small Bear* book to the whole class; I'd counted with her to one hundred at least a hundred times. She was a happy kindergartner who was doing a great job, and I was eager to hear all about it.

My conference was immediately after school. Rob was unable to join me so I went alone to the low, kidney-bean-shaped table at the back of Mrs. Murphy's room, while Emily played in the sandbox on the kindergarten playground, oblivious to the quiet judgments that were going on inside all those quite classrooms. I clutched Emily's first report card in my hand—a piece of paper that meant little to nothing. The schools don't want to give the kindergarteners proper grades because there's so little to grade, so instead they are given numbers—ones, twos, and threes, with twos being average. Emily had received all twos straight across the many categories, including pattern recognition and citizenship. This could easily be interpreted any way you chose, and I chose to believe that Emily was meeting expectations with a resounding ring of success. I didn't imagine that any child had gotten many ones or threes, let alone *all* ones or threes. I was feeling good.

Mrs. Murphy got out Emily's yellow writing folder, some pages of math she had done, and a stack of her artwork. She proceeded to explain that Emily was doing just fine, but then she said that Emily had gotten "itchy" when asked to count as high as she could, and that she had a chronic problem of not finishing her work in the allotted time. To illustrate this point, Mrs. Murphy showed me a page of handwritten *I*'s only halfway filled in.

I swallowed. I hadn't figured on this.

"Itchy?" I said.

"I think she was nervous," Mrs. Murphy explained. I nodded, putting together the idea of itchy and nervous in my mind. Emily was, after all, prone to eczema in the hot creases of skin at her knees and elbows, which did, now that I thought about it, give her something to do with her hands when she wasn't feeling perfectly comfortable.

"And what about the not finishing?" I asked, "What's that about?"

"She's not the only one who's slow, but many of the children are getting all their work done on time," Mrs. Murphy said, "It's one of the things we like to see them doing." Images swam into my mind of my volunteer hours in Emily's classroom, and I couldn't see the picture Mrs. Murphy had described. It didn't ring particularly true to me. I fought it, but all the same, I nodded—a plan for swooping in to fix the problem already emerging in my brain.

Then Mrs. Murphy talked about Emily's reading. She must have shown me the colorful Early Reader books and the lists of words that Emily had mastered, but I remember nothing beyond one comment Mrs. Murphy made—a comment she couldn't possibly have known would strike me straight to the core, but which couldn't have been better designed to cause me anxiety.

"I remember what an exceptional reader Carlyn was in kindergarten," she said. "She was reading *Frindle*—a book way above grade level—and I was testing her on her comprehension. I asked her what the phrase 'wasting time' meant and Carlyn said, 'It means what you're having me do now.' I'll never forget that."

I cringed. "She said THAT?' I cried, raising my hands to my face as if to deflect the embarrassment.

"She WAS a terrific reader," Mrs. Murphy went on. "Emily is still at the sounding-words-out stage. You probably never went through that with Carlyn. You'll just have to be patient and help Emily to make the sounds."

I had already *been* helping Emily make the sounds, just as I had helped Carlyn. What was Mrs. Murphy saying? That Emily wasn't as good a reader as Carlyn was and never would be, and all I could do was just sit by and bear witness? Although I'd had the exact same thought myself, this sounded preposterous spoken aloud by a teacher.

I must have gasped, because in the next moment Mrs. Murphy said, "Wait a minute! I had Carlyn in FIRST grade, didn't I? She wasn't reading *Frindle* in kindergarten! She was probably sounding out words, too."

But the damage was already done; the kernel of doubt about Emily's reading ability had popped inside me.

About this time, Emily was going through a phase where she was waking me up in the middle of the night almost every night, sometimes more than once. At first I thought the problem was nightmares, since Emily would come into my room complaining about bats and dragons and assorted other bad guys. I patiently reminded her that she was safe, fetched soothing glasses of water, rubbed her back, and explained how you can ask your brain to put monsters in tutus and dragons in party hats. After more than a month of this agonizing routine, my friend Lori suggested that perhaps Emily's waking up had nothing to do with monsters. Perhaps she just liked the company.

Perhaps she liked the attention. Perhaps she had developed a habit that had to be broken. Rob and I came up with a plan to get Emily to stop: For every night that Emily woke me up, she would have to spend an hour alone in her room the next day. I thought the design was perfect because it gave Emily a chance to rest and think about her actions, and it gave me a chance to recover.

Soon after we started this behavior-modification program, I began to notice that Emily was enjoying her time in her room. She was looking forward to it, in fact. I peeked in the door one day and saw her lounging on her bed surrounded by a pile of books. She was reading to her stuffed animals. She was pointing out pictures and words and quietly—very quietly—sounding out the words on the page.

No one was cheering her on, no one was applauding her efforts, no one was pushing her to go further, yet she was doing it—the very thing I had so hoped to see happen. I had never noticed before because I was looking for Carlyn's style of loud and public performance reading, but as soon as I understood the difference in their styles, it seemed that Emily really began to learn how to read.

PAYING ATTENTION

I'd like to say that I learned my lesson from Mrs. Murphy once and for all—the lesson of letting go, of stepping back, of seeing each of my girls for who they are. But I still struggle. I'm heartened by the fact that I don't seem to be alone. A few years ago, novelist Jane Smiley wrote an incandescent essay about motherhood called "Mothers Should," and near the end of it she wrote these lines about her daughter:

> Even after conceiving, bearing, birthing and rearing her, even after watching her and talking to her for almost 20 years, I would have to say, no, I don't know her. She comes fully equipped with her own self, which is other than mine, and is in some ways entirely outside my experience. But I remember quite well what it felt like not to be able to wait to see the faces of my babies. Now I would like to see their faces again and do it all over, not with an eye to winning or losing, but with an eye to paying better attention.

Twenty years, and Smiley still doesn't even feel like she knows her daughter. But she does know that her daughter is *not her.* I try to hold onto that fact, particularly when parent-teacher conferences come around.

12

Togetherness

One of my favorite descriptions about writing talks about the talent of the empty room—of sitting alone in a chair, staying in one place, putting in the time needed to get the words down on paper. I came across this description in an essay by writer Michael Ventura, who goes on to say that "before any issues of style, content or form can be addressed, the fundamental questions are: How long can you stay in that room? How many hours a day? How do you behave in that room? How often can you go back to it? How much fear (and, for that matter, how much elation) can you endure by yourself? How many years—*how many years*—can you remain alone in a room?"

Sounds a little like learning to read, doesn't it? Especially when you add in the part about how "every single word is full of secrets, full of associations, every word leads to another and another and another, down and down, through passages of dark and light." Everyone learning to read must practice the talent of the room. They have to learn how to just sit there, page after page after page, unlocking the secrets of the words in front of them. It takes time, and the breakthroughs usually come with little fanfare. The good news is that children don't normally have to endure it alone because the time is often spent in the presence of Mom and Dad.

One night a few weeks before school let out for winter break, Carlyn and I were taking turns trying to recite " 'Twas the Night Before Christmas" and Emily was curled up on the couch watching us, waiting for her bedtime stories. I'd been reading and hearing the poem my entire life, but I only had about five stanzas committed to memory, and not all of those in the correct order. The stanza that stumped me every time was the one where all the reindeer are named—"On Dasher, on Dancer, on Donder and Blitzen, on Comet and Cupid and Donder and . . . no, wait, it's Vixen next . . . or is it Blitzen? Does Blitzen come before Vixen?"

"Blitzen's first," Carlyn said. She stood and whizzed through the reindeer names. When she was done, Emily asked if I could read to her now.

"Let me just see if I can get the reindeer names," I said, gearing up to try the difficult lines again.

In a voice just barely under control, Emily said, "Mom, could you please stop and read me a bedtime story?"

"Mom," Carlyn protested, before I could form an answer, "you promised we'd memorize the poem!"

"I didn't promise we'd do it tonight," I argued.

"But you promised," she pushed.

At this point, Emily started to cry. "You never do anything with me!" she wailed. "You always do things with Carlyn."

I could see that she had a point.

"Carlyn," I said, fighting to keep my voice measured, "I've been doing this with you for a while and Emily's been very patient. We can work on it another night. Right now I'm going to stop and read Emily some stories."

"Fine," Carlyn said, and stormed out of the room.

Emily picked out a picture book about a mouse who makes a home in the straw of Jesus' manger. When we were done, she fished around in the pile of Christmas books and pulled out *Auntie Claus*. *Auntie Claus* is long. It demands a lot of enthusiastic reading to evoke the effervescent Auntie. It can be a tough choice when you're tired.

"Are you sure?" I asked, half hoping for something shorter and easier.

"I'm sure," she said, so I plunged in and read about Santa's stylish and mysterious New York relative.

Emily was in a good mood. She had gotten her way, and she was grateful for the small victory. She was focused, happy, and warm, snuggled under her purple-checked blanket. She let me point to the words of the text as I read, which she usually hated, and she sounded out the easy words I paused at without complaint and without, it seemed, much effort. I was cheered by her eagerness, and what had started out feeling like an obligation now felt like fun.

"Why don't we get *The Cat in the Hat?*" I suggested, when *Auntie Claus* was done. Emily's face creased with skepticism; the tip of her nose turned white.

"You'll love this," I promised. The cat himself has always given me the creeps—a scrawny, half-human, half-feline character who inexplicably appears at the door and forces his way inside—but I liked the schoolmarmish fish, the plucky twins, the whole idea of entertaining oneself on a rainy day with nothing but imagination, and all of this was wrapped up in simple sing-song rhymes. As I flipped to find the first page, Emily spotted the third page, on which the word "sit" is repeated four times and laid out across the paper like a playground slide.

"I want to read THAT page," she said.

"Perfect," I agreed, "I'll tell you when we get there."

I read the opening pages about the rain and the boredom, and when we got to the third page, Emily started in, slowly sounding out each word, then pausing to let the sounds settle together and make a word. The fourth word stumped her—for good reason.

"It's *could,*" I explained, "You don't hear the *L*."

"Why not?" she asked.

"It's just a silly rule," I said, trying not to betray the truly awful realities of the English language that would be coming her way—the fact that *home* and *come* do not rhyme; that the word that describes a sharp corner is not spelled *a-n-g-e-l;* and that there is a big difference between *affect* and *effect,* which even her mother, a writer, usually gets wrong. "There's no good reason for it. You just have to memorize words like that."

She nodded and went back to the start of the page and read it through with feeling and authority.

So all we could do was to
Sit!
   Sit!
      Sit!
         Sit!
And we did not like it.
Not one little bit.

"Let's do more pages," she suggested.

I was tired, but I didn't want to lose momentum.

We worked through the next pages, our mouths stretching out the sounds of the letters, but then we hit a page that had a few tricky words so I said, "Emily, you point and I'll read." I'd never done that before—given her control of the finger that points to the text—and it turned out to be a brilliant idea. She tapped each word, and if I got ahead of her, she stopped in objection. She went slow and fast, rushing and braking the speed according to her whims, and pursing her lips in a barely controlled smile the whole time. I played the good citizen reader to her text traffic cop, and together we read about three more pages.

I set the book down and when I looked up, Rob was standing in the kitchen with a video camera pointed directly at us.

"How long have you been there?" I cried. The camera was new—purchased to capture Carlyn's first swim meet. We'd never had a video camera of any kind. I wasn't used to being caught.

"Ten minutes," he answered, smiling.

I didn't have to ask what had made him decide that, of all the many moments Emily and I had sat together to read on the couch, *this* was the one worth capturing. It had everything—a mom and a daughter, a blanket and a book, and a series of happy words that slid down the page.

Emily and I were both exhausted by our effort. I carried her to her bed and tucked her under her purple blanket, but before I could get out of the room, Carlyn whispered, "I heard Emily reading *The Cat in the Hat*." She was throwing me a rope of reconciliation, so I took it. I motioned for Carlyn to be quiet, and for her to follow me to my room. We snuggled under the covers.

"*The Cat in the Hat* is perfect for her right now," I explained.

"I used to like *Hop on Pop*," Carlyn said.

"I remember that. You'd sit there and sound out the whole book, and it took *forever!*"

Carlyn smiled, happy to know that she had once pinned me down the exact same way Emily had just pinned me down. "I did?" she asked.

"Oh, yeah."

"I think this is the best book I've ever read," she announced, holding out *Where the Red Fern Grows*."

"Better than *Harry Potter?*"

"Yeah," she said, nodding her head.

"Better than *The Cat and the Hat?*"

"Mom!" she chided.

"Just checking," I said.

BEYOND THE BOOK

Lately I've started to notice how many times a day I say to my kids, "Come on. Hurry up. Get moving"—or some variation on that theme. I say it every morning at least a dozen times when we get ready for school, swim meets, soccer games, or Sunday school. Then I say it to them when they sit down to do their homework in the afternoon, and also when we sit down to eat dinner. (Emily is a v-e-r-y slow eater.) I say it to them when we're getting in and out of the car to run errands or to go to birthday parties or to go to friend's house for dinner. I say it when it's time to get out of the bath or ready for bed. About the only time I do not say it, in fact, is when we are reading. You simply can't hurry reading. So the sitting there, in and of itself, is sending a huge message to my kids: that there are times in the day when it's important to stop and slow down and spend time with each other that is free from hurry.

13

Grace

Over the long President's Day weekend, Rob and I took the
girls skiing up at Big Bear, the closest ski resort to Los Angeles.
We rented a tiny little cabin that seemed more like a playhouse.
It had a miniature refrigerator and a miniature stove, a bedroom
as big as a queen-size bed, and a living room that was taken up
by the futon when it was unfolded. After our second day of skiing, we all came back to the cabin exhausted and cold. It had
been raining on the hill—a particular threat to Southern California skiing—but we had skied, and we had skied hard. It was
only 4:00 P.M., but it felt like 10:00. We cranked up the heater,
built a fire in the tiny fireplace, and made popcorn and hot
chocolate. While the girls ate their snack, I climbed under the
blankets on the futon and cracked open *Where the Red Fern*

Grows, which Carlyn had asked me to read because it had made her cry and want to have a dog of her own.

I try to make sure that the books don't all flow one way in our family. I think the book-recommendation highway should be a two-way street. Kids know when we're trying to cram stuff down their throats, and they know when we're using outside resources—like a book—to speak on our behalf. I want Carlyn to read good writing. I want her to know the difference between good writing and popular writing. It's not that I don't value *Captain Underpants,* but I want her to tackle complexity so that she has that skill. To this end, I introduce her to Newberry Medal winners and classic American stories. She, on the other hand, wants me to understand how closely fairies, in her mind, mirror our own world, and so she gives me *The Fairy Rebel* to read. And when she told me I just HAD to read *The Elevator Family* because it was SOOOO funny, I read that book, too, trying to see what she thought was such a crack-up, trying to see *her.*

The theologian Ron Rolheiser wrote: "Nothing is better than being seen, noticed and appreciated by a significant other, especially when you are still young, unsure of yourself, and unsure of what you have to offer the world." I've found no better way to do that than by reading the books my children recommend.

Sometimes I struggle through the selections Carlyn gives me, but *Where the Red Fern Grows* was different: I was loving it. I was halfway through, and it was so riveting, heartfelt, and dramatic that I longed to lose myself in the story. I tuned out the after-ski chatter and the clinking spoons and the popcorn flying to the floor and continued to read. The next time I looked up, Carlyn had opened her book—Philip Pullman's *The Amber Spyglass*—and was reading beside me. Rob was looking through a stack of magazines he'd hauled from home, and Emily was still sipping her hot chocolate, spooning one marshmallow at a time, and staring at the fire. We had forgotten board games, pads of paper, decks of cards. We only had books and each other. While I waited for Emily to finish her hot chocolate, I kept reading to find out what happened in the deep dark woods of the Ozarks when Billy found his beloved dog trapped in the frozen river.

When Emily announced that she was done with her snack, I said, "Pick a book and come read next to me." She got out Richard Scarry's *What Do People Do All Day?* the book that had remained on the top of her favorite list for many months. It is a rich book, full of information about roads and carpentry and the mail, peopled with charming characters, packed with interesting words and funny situations; it is one of my favorites, too. She climbed onto the futon and started to look at the words and the pictures, and, to my surprise, did not ask me to read. I rubbed her back and returned to my book.

It startled me when Carlyn was the one to break the silence: "Mom," she whispered, "where are you?"

"Huh?" I asked, looking up.

"What's happening in the book? Where are you?" Carlyn repeated.

"Oh, well, I . . . he just saved Little Ann from the river."

"Oh," she said eagerly, "Mom, the best part is coming.

You're so close. It's . . . you won't believe it. Do you want me to find the page it's on?"

"No, don't tell me!" I insisted, I went back to my story. Emily continued to read quietly beside me. Rob worked through his magazines. The fire crackled.

"Where are you now?" Carlyn asked a minute later.

"Carlyn!"

"Sorry," she said.

I was amazed that Emily continued to look at her Richard Scarry book through these exchanges. She was content. She had found her own rhythm and her own joy right there on the futon in the miniature cabin on a rainy, late winter afternoon.

"I just want to know. I just have to know," Carlyn said. She leaned over me and hung her head over my shoulder so she could see the words on the page as I read them.

"You're so close!" she blurted. She reached out and paged ahead in my book.

"Carlyn," I said, laughing now, "go away!"

I reached the part I knew Carlyn was anticipating—the horrifying scene where a boy we are made to hate accidentally falls on an ax and slices open his own stomach. It's a brutal and bloody image, and you feel terribly sorry for the boy and for the hero of the story, who only moments ago was being tortured by the kid who now lies dying. I read it three times over, marveling at the gore, at the perfectly pitched drama, and at the fact that this was a scene permanently fixed in my nine-year-old daughter's brain.

When I closed the book, Carlyn was back by my side. "Wasn't that intense?" she asked.

"That was very intense," I agreed.

"Didn't you feel like you were right there watching it?" she said, and I agreed that I did. We spoke about how unfair it was, and how sad, and having gotten the common understanding she so desperately wanted, Carlyn went back to *The Amber Spyglass*.

I glanced around the little cabin, now dark with the night and lit by the fire. My whole family was there, and it felt like we were in a state of grace. I realized that it wasn't really about anyone's ability to read, and it wasn't about any of the books that were being read. It was about just being able to be together in a quiet room, at peace in each other's presence.

WHAT YOU GET WHEN YOU TURN OFF THE TV

Moments of family grace always seem to come when the TV is turned off, whether we're on a vacation, taking time to play a board game together, planting sunflower seeds in the garden, or driving in the car. Talk to anyone who has anything to do with inspiring kids to read, and you will hear them bemoan the amount of time kids spend watching TV. I don't know that a zero-TV-tolerance policy is necessary for raising readers (my kids watch their fair share of videos and Saturday morning cartoons), but limits are definitely key. For an inspiring story of a family who weaned itself off TV and reaped big rewards, read Katrina Kenison's *Mitten Strings for God*. For an analysis of the way TV watching can eat into a child's ability to imagine, to learn, and to read, go back to www.trelease-on-reading.com. While you're there, you can also read about the restored audiotape of a famous lecture that Wilson Rawls, author of *Where the Red Fern Grows*, gave about how self-doubt led him to burn the manuscript of his now-famous novel about a boy and his dogs.

14

Communion

If your kids love to read, one of the things they probably love about it is the chance to slow down, sit down, and be by themselves with their own imaginations. If *you* love to read, you know exactly why they crave this opportunity for quiet. I see my kids using reading as an antidote to their fast-paced lives. If they have a bad day at school or they're not feeling well or things have been rushing by at a furious pace, they will withdraw to their beds, slip under the covers, and lose themselves in a book. When they come back up for air, they are refreshed.

It is at this point in your child's reading career that you might stop reading aloud altogether. You might think that they don't need it anymore and that they may not even want it. But Jim Trelease insists that kids of all ages not only love to hear a story, but derive great benefit from it as well. There's something comforting about hearing the sound of another person telling a story, and while you listen, you can't help but learn new vocabulary, understand the reason for grammar, and soak up the ways that stories rise, fall, and teach us things about ourselves and our world.

This point was driven home recently in an article by Edward Rothstein, who was confessing his newfound addiction to books on tape. "I listen in the street, on the subway, exercising, cleaning, opening mail, eating, driving," he writes. No matter where he listens, he finds his reactions more direct and physical than they are when he is reading a book to himself in silence. Hearing a book read out loud allows the elements of the story to go straight to your bones.

Emily and I are still happily at the height of the read-aloud book stage (we're working our way through Beverly Cleary's delightful *Ramona* series), but Carlyn is so often immersed in her own books that it's getting harder and harder to entice her with the slower pace of a story read aloud. I try to occasionally present books that I think would be fun to read aloud to both girls, and they occasionally accept, and we have the pleasure of reading a book in common.

This happened in the spring of Emily's year in kindergarten when I read the kids *Charlotte's Web*. I chose that book because I'd heard a story about a young mother dying of breast cancer who spent her final week of life reading to her children. I'd heard a lot of stories about breast cancer that year because I'd survived the disease and written a book about it that came out that fall. Wherever I went to speak about my book, women came up to me to share their stories about living and dying. You can never hear enough stories about surviving, but it was the stories about dying that stuck with me—particularly the stories about young mothers.

I was reasonably certain that I wasn't going to die, but when you have an illness that could kill you, you can't help but contemplate it. I found myself frequently lapsing into daydreams about my own death. How would I say good-bye to my children? What would I do in my last days? The story about the mother who chose to read gave me the details my imagination needed to fill in the blanks. For seven days, this mom read aloud from *Charlotte's Web*. She read about the girl, Fern, who saves the runt pig; the spider, Charlotte, who saves the grown pig; and finally, she read the heartbreaking scene where Charlotte reveals that these are her last days by explaining to Wilbur the point that has escaped him in his desperate bid to live forever: "We're born, we live a little, we die." Charlotte dies in the next chapter "knowing her children were safe," and I like to imagine that the young mother I'd heard about did, too.

For more than a year after I heard the story, I was haunted by the image of a terminally ill mom in bed reading to her children. I kept turning the story over and over in my mind—how selfless the mom was; how confident; and how, in the midst of so much pain and grief, she was able to settle on a book—just *one* book!—to deliver her final message. Finally, in an act of solidarity, I read *Charlotte's Web* to my children to see how the whole thing felt.

My kids knew the plot from the movie, but it's a beautiful story beautifully told and we all enjoyed listening to it. When we got near the end of the book, I read the heading of Chapter 21: "Last Day."

"This is where Charlotte dies," Carlyn announced.

"It's a sad ending, isn't it?" I said.

"Yeah," my kids said.

But then, after a moment, Emily piped up. "I think it's a happy ending," she argued, "because Wilbur gets three new friends."

I had picked *Charlotte's Web* to help myself make sense of a world where young mothers could die. That was the way books worked for me, how they spoke to me, how I enjoyed them. I was focused on the spider dying and her children flying off to make their own place in the world. But Emily experienced *Charlotte's Web* in a different way. She heard a message about the pig's happiness, about friendship; and because we had read the book together, we were able to share our collective wisdom.

ONE DAD'S STORYTIME SECRET

My friend Peggy Eysenbach is the daughter of a man who would win the Nobel Prize for reading aloud, if such an award were given. This man had five children, and he read to each one of them for half an hour every night throughout their entire childhood. When his children had children, he would sometimes purchase the books they were reading at home so he could call them long distance and read them a chapter over the phone.

Peggy's stories about her dad inspired me to write a story about a parent reading aloud to his child. I'm writing it down here so that it might inspire you, too:

Peggy's Storytime Secret

Two months after the start of first grade, Peggy discovered she could read anything she wanted to read, and for two months after that, she pretended she couldn't.

She pretended she couldn't read the chalkboard.

She pretended she couldn't read her homework.

She even pretended she couldn't read the flavors at the ice-cream store.

She couldn't let her teacher know she could read because her teacher would tell her mom.

She couldn't let her mom know she could read because her mom would tell her dad.

And she couldn't let her dad know she could read because he might never read to her again.

Storytime with her dad was Peggy's favorite part of the day. After he read picture books to the baby and poems to the twins, he tapped on Peggy's door, sat down on her bed, and asked her where they'd left off the night before.

"Sarah just got locked in the attic," she'd call out, or "Reepicheep just fell into the water."

Her dad would nod, pull her close, and start reading the next chapter in his deep and rumbling voice.

He never got up while he was reading—not to get the twins another drink of water, not even to answer the phone. For that half hour every day, her dad was hers alone.

One day just after Christmas, Peggy and her family were on their way to the science museum. While her dad drove in circles searching for the parking lot, the baby began to scream and the twins began to fight.

On the third lap around the same block, Peggy couldn't help herself. "Turn, Dad!" she yelled. "The sign says museum parking is that way."

"Nice reading, Peggy," her mom said, and looked at her in a funny way.

Her dad didn't say anything until they were standing underneath the towering T-Rex in the museum lobby.

"Why don't you read the sign to us, Peggy," he challenged.

"It's a replica," she mumbled, "by a pale-on-tologist. It's carnivo-rous."

That night when her dad was reading picture books to the baby and poems to the twins, Peggy hid under her sheets.

She crammed Kleenex in her ears.

Fiercely, she hummed herself a lullaby.

When her dad came in and sat down on her bed, she peered out from under the sheets.

"*CAN YOU HEAR ME?*" he asked.

Peggy smiled miserably and pulled the Kleenex out of her ears. She stared at the crumpled tissue in her hands.

"Now," her dad said, as he picked up their book from the bedside table and turned to the next chapter, "Where'd we leave off last night?"

15

Jealousy

I'm not one of those mothers who wish their children could stay small forever. Despite the obvious pleasures of life with a baby, I thought it was really hard work, and I looked forward to the time when the job would be less about fulfilling the physical needs of my kids and more about guiding their emotional, physical, and spiritual development. I had no idea how, as soon as your children can put on their own pajamas and brush their own teeth, they start pulling away from you—in small ways at first, but in ways that feel immense and inevitable.

Books give you a powerful way to stay connected, which is why I tried really hard to keep reading aloud to my kids even after they could read themselves. Even on nights when we can't sit down together for dinner or nights when we've been angry at each other or nights when the phone has rung too many times, there's been too much homework, and we've spent half an hour looking for soccer socks, we can still take at least a little time to sit down together and read. It grounds us. It gives us a common experience to talk about and refer to.

I can sense when that connection starts to slip. It happened not too long after the lovely *Charlotte's Web* experience, when Carlyn was in the fifth grade. Rob was reading her Jules Verne's classic *Twenty Thousand Leagues Under the Sea*. He had been waiting a long time to read it to her because it had been one of the books he most remembered from his childhood, and they were having a grand time. They sat night after night in the living room reading the adventure, and whenever he stopped, no matter how long they had been going, Carlyn begged for him to read more.

I was not part of their small society, and I was jealous. The last three books I had tried to read out loud to Carlyn hadn't worked. She thought they were dumb. She invoked the three-chapter rule. And I had convinced myself that her read-aloud days were over—and with them, the sweet connection of sitting together and sharing a story.

But here was Rob, coming up with a book she adored, with the promise of many more to follow. "Dad's going to read me *Around the World in Eighty Days*" next, Carlyn announced, as *Twenty Thousand Leagues Under the Sea* was coming to a close.

"Not immediately," Rob jumped in to correct. It's not easy to give up forty-five minutes of prime-time after-dinner hours to a giant squid. He would read *Around the World in Eighty Days,* but not right away.

"Maybe I could read you something next," I suggested.

"You don't pick very exciting books, Mom," Carlyn said, apologetically.

Oh, how our kids can stab us in the heart!

I wanted to yell, "That's not true!" I wanted to beg and plead for her to give me another chance. I knew that all I would get in response to this emotional display were rolled eyeballs. So very calmly I asked, "Will you let me try again?"

Carlyn raised her eyebrows in doubt of my ability to find something appealing. "OK," she said, her voice dripping with skepticism.

I spent three hours at the bookstore in search of a book that would work. I tried to think of Carlyn's love of other worlds and magic, of adventure and fierce action, and must have picked up a dozen books that would have qualified, but the thing was that I'd made that mistake before with *The Hobbit* and *The Dark Is Rising*. All the elements Carlyn liked were in those books, but they didn't add up to a likeable whole for her. Sometimes just having the right qualifications wasn't enough. A book needed something else to catch on—something I found difficult to pin down. How could I even attempt to define what that something was for someone else when I knew I would be very hard pressed to define it for myself? All I knew was that I believed I could sense it when I saw it, so I finally decided my best bet was to simply pick a book I thought I would like. I picked four paperbacks from the shelf, using the same system I use for picking most of my own books: I had heard it mentioned somewhere; I liked the cover; the story sounded interesting; or when I flipped open to the text, the paragraph I read rang with the particular sound of an author on a roll.

I presented the books to Carlyn. She picked each one up, read the back covers, and settled on Sharon Creech's *Walk Two Moons,* a road trip story with a thirteen-year-old protagonist, who has more than her fair share of secrets to tell.

We started reading. When we got to the end of the third chapter, I gently asked if she wanted to stop, and she gently said, "No, keep reading, Mom."

Halfway through the book, we were both hooked. As we got toward the end, we were aghast at the surprising turn of events that came one right after another. I kept putting the book down on the table to take it all in before turning the page, and Carlyn would yell, "Mom, don't stop!"

"That was a *great* book," Carlyn proclaimed, when we finished the last page, and then she added, "I don't know why I liked it because it's not like what I usually like."

"I don't know why you like it," I said, "but I know why *I* liked it."

"Why's that?" she asked—an earnest, adultlike question coming out of my little girl's mouth.

I could have said something about the quirky characters, the pressing questions, the pace of the journey, the real-life dilemmas that were not easily solved, the hilarious dialogue, or the beautifully written sentences, but those were merely descriptions of what made the book sophisticated. Why I liked it was much simpler, and it was why I so often read, and why reading can connect us, and why I want to keep reading aloud to my oldest child as she keeps getting older and the task keeps getting harder:

"Because," I said, "we got to get into someone else's head."

I have jealousy to thank for giving me a second read-aloud life with Carlyn. Seeing my husband read to my daughter so naturally and so easily goaded me into action. It rekindled my passion. The next time Carlyn or Emily rejects three books in a row, I won't be so quick to give up.

BOY STYLE/GIRL STYLE

I admire Rob for making the time to read to our kids. He could easily have left the task to me—as well as all the pleasure—since it was so clearly my special area of interest. He could also have become a reader worker-bee, reading the books I suggested at the times I suggested and in the manner I suggested. Instead, he caught the spirit of the whole read-aloud impulse and found a way to make it his own. It was Rob who thought of the idea of reading *National Geographic* captions to the kids (Emily loves the animal stories), reading the sports page to them the morning after a big game (Carlyn loves the Lakers), and reading Jules Verne (Rob relished the chance to revisit a childhood favorite). He naturally did what I did with such fretful concern: He read the things he liked that he thought the kids would like. In this manner, he and our girls found a reading style that worked for them.

Would things have been any different in our house had we had two boys instead of two girls? I doubt it. I would have still cared as much about books as I do, and Rob would still have caught the spirit the way he did, and we would still have chosen things to read according to what we liked and according to the interests of our kids.

We have lots of friends who have both boys and girls, and they are always stunned at how early and strong the doll-truck division of interest kicks in. While it's true that a boy who loves to play with skip loaders is naturally going to adore *Mike Mulligan and the Steam Shovel*, he may also adore *Madeline*. A character who falls off a bridge into the river, gets her appendix out, and hides a dog in her bed has an appeal that's pretty universal. It's just that the boy might commit the fabulous lines of Madeline's tale to heart instead of asking for the doll for Christmas. When a book is good—think Harry Potter—it doesn't matter if you're a boy or a girl, a mom or a dad. We all want to lose ourselves in a good story; we all want to feel what it's like, just for a little while, to get inside someone else's head.

16

Perspective

The thing I love about getting older is that I get a sense of perspective about how things fit together and what really matters. I now understand exactly why people say they wouldn't go back to being sixteen again or why they wouldn't go back to the years when their children were small, even though those are some of the most memorable and cherished times of all: You'd lose the wisdom. Sometimes it doesn't even take very much distance for me to see how I have stumbled, and how I can be a better parent to my two girls—more supportive, less suffocating; more patient, less frantic. It is fitting that I came to this point of perspective about reading and children by means of a picture book.

In the last weeks of kindergarten, Emily checked a book out from the library called *Five Creatures,* by Emily Jenkins. At first this looked like a simple picture book about cats, but *Five Creatures* is the result of an exercise author Emily Jenkins did one day on a whim. She made a list of all the creatures that lived in her house—a child, two adults, and two cats—and tried to think of all the things they had in common. On each page of the picture book, the illustration depicts the places where the five creatures intersect and diverge—over their interest in eating fish, their willingness to take a bath, their ability to reach high cupboards. It's a clever idea, a kind of Venn diagram for kids, and Emily adored it. It appealed to the logical part of her brain. On each page of the book, you have to stop and shift your mind to figure out which creature belonged in the group being described.

Emily's favorite page in *Five Creatures* was a full spread at the end of the book with the text, "Five creatures who love birds, but not all in the same way." It was the only instance in the book where all five creatures agreed on any one thing. For two weeks I stared at this page every night at Emily's bedtime, reading the words and examining the illustration. The mom is shown lying in a hammock gazing at birds flying overhead. The dad is examining birds high in the sky through a pair of binoculars. The cats are gleefully chasing birds across the lawn. And the little girl is tossing out seeds to feed a small group of birds who have gathered around her.

This illustration perfectly captured my hard-won understanding of the place books and reading play in our family. I tried to stalk the pleasures of reading, capture them, and hand them as a gift to my children, tied up with a bow. But in the end, I saw that this isn't the way passion is passed along.

On Mother's Day, the year Carlyn was in the fourth grade,

she asked me to come into her room for one last hug, and when I did, she told me I was the greatest mom in the world. She also apologized for any difficulty she had caused me over her nine years and thanked me for all the support I had given her, particularly for being on the swim team.

Swimming is Rob's sport—though he is as quick to point out that he had nothing to do with Carlyn's interest in it as he is to proclaim how tickled he is that she's doing it. It was a lifeguard and a swim teacher one summer at our tennis club who told Carlyn that she had the potential to be fast, and that was all she needed to hear. She joined the team, started to swim, and has not stopped since.

I knew so little about competitive swimming that at Carlyn's first swim meet I had to ask another parent if the twentyfive-yard race was one length of the pool or two. I had no idea if the times Carlyn posted in any event were good or bad. Instead of watching the clock as my daughter swam down the lane, I just watched all the girls in the heat, brown and strong, as they churned through the water full of determination. They were so beautiful. As Carlyn's first season wore on, my expertise increased slightly, but not by much. When Carlyn was disqualified in a breaststroke event, I could not comment on her kick or her turn or her arm motions, the way some other parents could. I could only console her and tell her when her next event was and cheer as loudly as I could. On Mother's Day, Carlyn did not thank me for my support of her reading—for the endless trips to the library, the dollars spent at the bookstore, and the pages read out loud. She thanked me for supporting her doing what *she* loved.

I got the message, finally, loud and clear. The passion a parent feels for something can show up anywhere in the child's life. It's not the object of the passion that matters, but the passion itself. My children will know by my example the value inherent in loving something, in believing in it, and in throwing yourself into it whole hog. And no matter what passion they take on as their own, I'm proud and delighted to know that it will be enriched and enhanced by their ability to read with ease and with feeling.

A Few Books in Particular

Last summer I hired a high school senior to help me with some work. Her name is Blaire. She had been editor of her school newspaper and was on her way to college at Berkeley. She is, in other words, a smart cookie. Blaire's mother happened to be out of the country for several months to care for an ailing relative, and because Blaire was still only seventeen *she couldn't check books out of the public library*. She didn't have a library card; and without her mother's signature, she couldn't get one. Blaire stood in my living room and said to me, "I have two months with nothing to do, and I have nothing to read!"

We went to my bookshelf, which holds only a tiny fraction of the books I have read and loved, and I started pulling books off the shelf. "You must read this," I said, pulling down a novel, "and this, and this, and this."

Blaire left that day with seven books, and she left *me* with the satisfaction of having known her and known those books well enough to recommend. Other than reading itself, there is nothing more satisfying to a book lover.

It's hard to replicate that experience on paper, but I have to say that trying it has been enormously fun—so fun, in fact, that I heartily recommend the exercise. Design a few categories of the kinds of books you read, and then start listing books under each category. See if you can keep each list to under ten, just to make it more challenging. It's a terrific, humbling, wonderful activity. Below are my categories, and my lists:

Great Books to Give for a Baby Shower

• *The Read-Aloud Handbook* by Jim Trelease. This book not only presents an inspiring argument for reading aloud, it has list after list of what to read, when, and why. Someone gave me this book when Carlyn was born, and I can honestly say that it was my favorite baby gift. It has lasted the longest, for one thing, and has had an immeasurable impact on my whole family.

• *Goodnight Moon* by Margaret Wise Brown. Everyone loves this book for good reason. It never loses its gentle charm no matter how many times you read it—and as anyone who owns it knows, you will read it a lot.

• *Owl Babies* by Martin Waddell. Three fluffy, wise little owls wait for their mommy to come back to the nest—and she *comes*. It's all a human baby needs to know, and it's told with such reassuring language and lilting rhythm, they will believe it every time you read it. My favorite part is how Bill, the smallest of the three owls, says, "I want my mommy!" over and over again until, on the last page when the mommy owl has returned, he changes his refrain to, "I love my mommy."

• *Babybug, Ladybug, Spider,* or *Cricket* magazines. These magazines are well written, colorful, seasonal, engaging, and wonderful in every way. There are no advertisements—just stories, comics, and a few puzzles and games. Get *Babybug* for the new baby, and one of the other titles for older siblings. Available at www.cricketmag.com.

• *Brown Bear, Brown Bear, What Do You See?* by Bill Martin Jr. and Eric Carle. The simplest possible repetition and a surprise on every page make this the perfect first picture book. In preschool, my kids both made their own versions on construction paper with pictures of friends and family. We still have them.

• *Poetry by Heart: A Child's Book of Poems to Remember* compiled by Liz Attenborough. There are plenty of terrific books of poems and almost any one you choose will probably become a favorite because poems and kids just seem to go together. My family loves Shel Silverstein's collections for their loopy inventiveness, but we go back to *Poetry by Heart* again and again because the art is so inviting and because there are so many poems that are easy to read and remember. It offers both short and long poems, silly and serious poems, and new and classic.

• *Where's Spot?* by Eric Hill. An endlessly entertaining book for a little kid. You lift the flaps, you get to chant, "No" whenever you don't find the dog, and in the end, you find the dog. You can give someone their first copy of *Where's Spot?* and leave them to buy the replacements they are sure to need.

• *Book!* by Kristine O'Connell George. A toddler receives a book for a gift and explores all the many joys it offers. A magical celebration of the simple pleasures of books.

Picture Books That Are Just Plain Fun to Read Aloud

- *The Seven Silly Eaters* by Mary Ann Hoberman. Rhymes that take on a life of their own, a hilarious story, a satisfying ending, and incredibly detailed illustrations combine to make this a book I never tire of reading. It always cracks me up.

- *Mrs. Biddlebox* by Linda Smith. This is a brand-new favorite, with illustrations by Marla Frazee, who also did the pictures for *The Seven Silly Eaters*. (She's clearly a genius.) I ran across this book in a little bookshop near my house and laughed so hard at the witchy main character and the funk she was in that I just had to bring it home. Mrs. Biddlebox gets up on the wrong side of the bunk and there's a danger she'll be cranky all day, but she finds a way to make something good of the day—quite literally. Within fifteen minutes of this book coming into our house, Mrs. Biddlebox became part of our shared language, as in "You're crankier than Mrs. Biddlebox!"

- *Olivia* by Ian Falconer. Not all great picture books rhyme! The ideas about kids and how they behave are so dead-on accurate and the illustrations are so funny that this book can change my mood from black to white in five minutes. It's always a pleasure to turn the page and see Olivia trying on outfits or splattering paint on her wall.

- " *'Twas the Night Before Christmas.*" Are there any words in the English language more fun to say than these? Every December I'm convinced anew.

- *Tuesday* by David Wiesner. A wordless picture book that's fun to read aloud? Well, it's impossible not to make commentaries—and croaks—as frogs take flight in this book.

- *Where the Wild Things Are* by Maurice Sendak. Well, yes, it's a timeless classic and has been praised up and down for everything from the evocative illustrations of monsters to the economy of words, but the thing is, it's just so much fun to read. Sendak seems to tell you exactly where to pause and breath and emphasize certain words. I always feel like I'm singing a duet with the pictures—I talk and then they talk, and it all works out beautifully every time.

Picture Book Authors
You Can Always Count On

You can go to these authors in the library or the bookstore, take home anything they've written, and be very happy with your choice. There are dozens of other such authors, and it's fun for kids to take ownership of a few for themselves—which is why you should always say the name of the author before you read a story. Odds are that the kids will put two-and-two together about who's written which book long before you do.

• Cynthia Rylant must be the most prolific modern children's book author, and I am very happy she is. All of her books are written with style, humor, and honesty. They seem to go straight to the heart of what's important in a young kid's life. There's Henry and Mudge and the Mr. Putter and Tabby series and Poppleton, but don't miss *When I Was Young in the Mountains* or *Dog Heaven*. We don't even have a dog, but *Dog Heaven* has become one of the most important theological texts in our home. My kids and I share a vision because of this book—that heaven is a place where you come into the fullness of your being and get all your favorite treats besides.

• Maurice Sendak. I think everything Sendak touches is considered a classic. *In the Night Kitchen, Chicken Soup with Rice, Alligators All Around, Where the Wild Things Are* . . . the list goes on and on.

• Robert McCloskey. McCloskey is the Norman Rockwell of picture books. His stories are all so simple and straightforward, evoking times that seem infinitely reassuring. *Blueberries for Sal, One Morning in the Maine,* and *Lentil* have all been well thumbed in our household.

• Rosemary Wells. The McDuff books are adorable; Max and all his pals are adorable; Wells's *Mother Goose* and *Rogers and Hammerstein* books are adorable. Even when she's not adorable—as in the gorgeous retelling of *Lassie*—Rosemary Wells is fabulous.

• Richard Scarry. His big books, *The Very Best Word Book Ever* and *What Do People Do All Day?* as well as some of the smaller stories, have probably been held more hours, overall, than any other books in our house. The characters are sweet, the stories goofy, and the words clearly written next to each illustration. Both my kids learned to count by the illustrations on the inside covers.

Books to Read Aloud
on a Rainy Day by Firelight

It's not that we ever really spend a rainy day sitting around reading books. We live in Southern California, for one thing, and it never rains here. We also rarely have a day with nothing to do. But I think of these books as comfort food—books whose effect is so soothing, and so comforting, and so uplifting that if you DID have a rainy day with absolutely nothing to do, you WOULD pick these books to read in front of the fire.

• *Charlotte's Web* by E. B. White. Poll a group of people who read, and the majority of them are likely to cite *Charlotte's Web* as an early and lasting favorite. After you read the book, find the recorded version, which was narrated by E. B. White himself. It's a treat for a long car ride.

• *Ella Enchanted* by Gail Carson Levine. If you ever wanted to rewrite *Cinderella* so that it wasn't all about the prince saving the day but more about Cinderella saving herself, this book will have you cheering. It's so clever, and it's got ogres and trolls and beasts galore.

- *From the Mixed-up Files of Mrs. Basil E. Frankweiler* by E. L. Konigsburg. What a great fantasy—to run away to the Metropolitan Museum of Art, gather money from the fountain, and sleep in those old, off-limits beds. The kids in this story actually do it.

- *The Wheel on the School* by Meindert DeJong. You'll need a lot of rainy days to get through this book, but it's completely delightful and far more action packed than it sounds. It won a Newberry in 1954. It follows a group of Danish schoolchildren who challenge themselves to figure out why the storks stopped nesting in their town and to find a way to bring them back.

- *Walk Two Moons* by Sharon Creech. This story held the attention of my daughter, who insisted that she wouldn't like anything that didn't have magic and fantasy on every page. It's beautifully written, perfectly paced, *funny* in a quirky way, and one of those books with a sad ending that somehow doesn't leave you feeling sad. We have had so much fun reading *Walk Two Moons* that we can't wait to get to *Chasing Redbird,* the follow-up book.

- *Where the Red Fern Grows* by Wilson Rawls. I really did read this book on a rainy afternoon. See page 88.

The First Series My Kids Loved to Read on Their Own

* *Mr. Putter and Tabby Paint the Porch* by Cynthia Rylant. There are about a dozen Mr. Putter and Tabby titles and they're all wonderful. Mr. Putter is the old man you'd pick to live next door, if you could, and Tabby is his old cat. They live next door to Mrs. Teaberry, who is the old woman you'd pick to live next door, if you could, and Zach is her old dog. The misadventures of these gentle folk are familiar and hilarious. *Mr. Putter and Tabby Paint the Porch* is our favorite because it's the funniest—although *Mr. Putter and Tabby Pick the Pears* features underwear used as a slingshot, which is pretty nifty, too.

* *Henry and Mudge in the Sparkle Days* by Cynthia Rylant . . . again. Henry's a boy, Mudge is his big dog, and in these early chapter books, they have every kind of adventure together, from thunderstorms to visiting cousins. My kids both loved these books, but Emily in particular latched onto them. She brought home five or six from the library each week for several months running, and I (almost!) never got tired of them.

Series That Hooked My Kids
a Little Later

- The Ramona Series (*Ramona the Pest; Beezus and Ramona; Ramona Quimby, Age 8,* etc.) by Beverly Clearly. Cleary is among the most beloved children's authors because she really gets the kids right. You are right there, waiting to go to kindergarten, and right there on the first day of school, and right there in every grade thereafter. Kids love to hear that they are not the only ones who are desperate to be the teacher's pet, who have been sent to the principal's office, who have thrown up in class, or who know that there is no tougher job—or more wondrous job—than being a kid. Even when I read these books to Emily, Carlyn will inch her way over to listen. If your kids don't care for Ramona, try Cleary's Ralph S. Mouse books.

- The American Girl Series. These books about girls throughout history are formulaic but fun for early and middle elementary school. The girls tackle some serious issues and learn some serious lessons, which kids love to hear about. The best part, however, are the bits and pieces about life during other times—the fact that there were no cars or that sugar was rationed.

• Everything by Roald Dahl. *James and the Giant Peach, Charlie and the Chocolate Factory, Fantastic Mr. Fox, The Witches, The Twits, Matilda,* etc. Though not technically a series, Dahl's books have such a distinct writing style that they naturally go together. The craziness of the characters and the setups act like magnets to readers who are ready to take flight.

• Everything by Judy Blume. *Fudge-A-Mania, Super Fudge* (and now there's *Double Fudge*), *Otherwise Known as Sheila the Great, Tales of a Fourth Grade Nothing,* etc. Blume's books introduce some slightly more complicated emotions and relationships, which kids begin to welcome when they can read this much text.

What Carlyn Turned to
After Harry Potter

- The Redwall series by Brian Jacques. Animals are the characters here, but there are plenty of battles as they fight for good and evil. Carlyn goes back to these books more than she does to Harry, and she has gone back to Harry a good deal.

- *His Dark Materials Trilogy* by Philip Pullman, including *The Golden Compass, The Subtle Knife,* and *The Amber Spyglass.* Carlyn was obsessed by this series for half a year. Be forewarned that some parents object to Pullman's ideas about God.

- Eva Ibbotson's books, including *Island of the Aunts, Which Witch?,* and *The Secret of Platform 13,* are rich, complex fantasies with plenty of magic to go around.

- *The Chronicles of Narnia* series by C. S. Lewis. There's magic, lots of mysterious creatures, adventures, and far-off destinations.

Books My Friend Paula, Who Is a Professional Storyteller and Who Reads More Than Anyone I Know, Insists Must Be Read by Every Kid on the Planet*

* *Dinosaur Bob* by William Joyce. Also *Santa Calls*. Paula is an artist, in addition to a storyteller, and Joyce is her favorite illustrator. Check out the gorgeous illustrations and you'll know why.

* *Trashy Town* by Andrea Griffing Zimmerman and David Clemesha. Mr. Gilly has a ton of trash to pick up and the kids know it and love having to remind Mr. Gilly on every page of all the work there is to be done.

* *Piggy in the Puddle* by Charlotte Pomerantz. Paula is partial to pig books, and this one is a treat. Hilarious, loopy rhymes.

* *Everything* by Eleanor Estes, Edward Eager, E. Nesbit, E. L. Konisburg, and Ray Bradbury.

*Note: This is only a partial list. Paula's list was twelve pages long.

• *Harriet the Spy* by Louise Fitzhugh. Paula called me back in a fit of panic because she had forgotten this book on her original list. "It was the first book I loved," she says. "I can't believe I would forget it! Please put it on my list!"

• *The Hitchhiker's Guide to the Galaxy* by Douglas Adams. This is a book that's usually found on adult reading lists, but Paula says that she has never found a kid who didn't love it. It's hilarious. She claims it convinced one boy who said he hated to read to become a reader.

• *A Wrinkle in Time* by Madeline L'Engle. "Of course," Paula says, "there's no question. I mean, you absolutely must include *A Wrinkle in Time.*" It's classic science fiction fantasy.

Books I Wish I Could Convince My Kids to Read

- *Anne of Green Gables* by Lucy Maud Montgomery. Anne is just so wonderfully *plucky*.

- *Caddie Woodlawn* by Carol Ryrie Brink. I loved Caddie when I was a kid, and my kids just won't even give her the time of day.

- *Riders of the Pony Express* by Ralph Moody. It's out of print, so it's only available at good libraries, but I just adored the action, the adventure, the intrigue, the sense of place. It's sitting right here on the bookshelf, and no one will pick it up.

- *Little Women* by Louisa May Alcott. This novel does so many things so well, and it's so tragic and so wonderful and leads to so many of the great English romance novels. At least there's plenty of time for this one to catch on and stick.

• *The Adventures of Sherlock Holmes* by Arthur Conan Doyle. I used to love to try to outwit the great detective, even though I was really bad at that kind of logic. I think Carlyn would get a kick out of it if she could get past the slightly archaic English, but she's been firm in her disinterest. I think she thinks it's an adult book that I'm trying to foist on her—as if there's some definable difference between a good book for young people and a good book for everyone else. There will come a time when Carlyn reads a book that bridges the difference—something like *Call of the Wild*—that can't exactly be called a children's book but seems far too thrilling to be considered adult; and she will then realize that all of the world's literature is hers to curl up with and read.

• *The Gift of the Magi* by O. Henry. If I *were* to try to foist an adult story on my kids, this is the kind of story I would choose. It's not just that it's got gorgeous language, a perfect structure, and a beautiful message, although those things don't hurt the cause. It's that it's a story that makes the small details of human interaction come alive, and those are the books that resonate the deepest for me. I think we gravitate as adults toward the kinds of books we loved as children, and I still can't help wishing that my children will grow up to love some of the same kinds of stories that I do.

Web Site

For more information about raising a reader, and to contact Jennie Nash about speaking engagements, visit www.jennienash.com.

Acknowledgments

Many thanks to my editor, Jane Rosenman, who's given me the priceless gift of an ongoing editorial relationship; the terrific team at St. Martin's, including Ethan Friedman, Beth Gissinger, Dori Weintraub, John Murphy, and genius cover artist Krista Olson, my wonderful agent, Betsy Amster; Kristine Breese, who went way beyond the call of friendship to help me find the shape of this narrative; Paula Strawn for the drawing of the girl in the chair and all her enthusiasm; Bridget O'Brian, Lori Logan, Denise Honaker, Jo Giese, Michelle Murphy, Barbara Abercrombie, and Peggy Eysenbach, who read drafts at various stages, talked with me about books, and offered support and insights; Penny Markey at the Los Angeles County Public Library and Kristine O'Connell George for their generosity and their connections; and Emily, Carlyn, and Rob Robertson, for filling my life with so many good stories.

About the Author

Jennie Nash is the author of *Altared States: Surviving the Engagement* and *The Victoria's Secret Catalog Never Stops Coming and Other Lessons I Learned from Breast Cancer*. She lives with her husband and two children in Los Angeles, California.